D0188834

INDELIBLE IN THE HIPPOCAMPUS

McSWEENEY'S
SAN FRANCISCO

Copyright © 2019

Cover by Sunra Thompson

All rights reserved, including right of reproduction in whole or in part, in any form.

Some names have been changed to protect individuals' privacy.

McSweeney's and colophon are registered trademarks of McSweeney's, an independent publisher based in San Francisco.

Printed in the United States.

ISBN 978-1-944211-71-4

10 9 8 7 6 5 4 3 2 1

www.mcsweeneys.net

**Deschutes
Public Library**

"*Indelible in the Hippocampus* makes permanently exterior the seemingly inexhaustible ways that women of all kinds have been aggressed upon. Whether it is a historic account of a woman of color defying social expectations by speaking publicly of rape by white men or the most personal, intimate self-contained dialogue remembering and processing a sexual boundary violation, this valuable anthology is a proper danger to patriarchal silencing. Our #MeToo stories are empirical method investigation. They are evidence. They are important."

—Ashley Judd

"Bracing and urgent... the writers offer a sense of communal feeling, bravery, and triumph." —*Publishers Weekly*

"This anthology functions as an empowered testament and treatise, a book for anyone interested in social justice... belongs on campuses and in community conversations... Not just candid and clear revelations of abuse, but powerful demands for justice." —*Kirkus* (starred review)

"This book is like a tinderbox in my hand, ready to start a fire. I'm so excited it exists." —Jami Attenberg, author of *All Grown Up*

"At once illuminating and poignant, these writings both shatter and heal." —Tabitha St. Bernard-Jacobs, The Women's March

"*Indelible in the Hippocampus* is one of the most profound and moving books I've read in quite some time. Personal, political, and artfully written essays, poems and fiction. Raw in its honesty and fearless with its insights. This book read as a revelation to me, and I was grateful for it. It should be read by anyone, everyone."

—Victor LaValle, author of *The Changeling*

"This anthology does so much to humanize, again, the stories that have emerged from the #MeToo movement, already much dismissed and pushed off to the margins. And while that would be enough, it is more than that. There are many beloved writers here, in discussions of the movements that led to this moment, the ways in which too many of us have struggled alone with what happened to us, the legacy of the culture that created these assaults, and inspiration for taking action on restorative justice. This is a book for those losing heart, those already fighting, and those just finding their voice. Which means give it to everyone."

—Alexander Chee, author of *How to Write an Autobiographical Novel*

"Indelible in the Hippocampus is a vital act of witnessing, a fortification for the body and the spirit, a reckoning with violences that belong to both the present and the past. 'Speaking lights a candle in a room inside us,' Gabrielle Bellot writes. This is a book that is going to light so many candles, in so many rooms."

—Laura van den Berg, author of *The Third Hotel*

INDELIBLE
IN THE
HIPPOCAMPUS

WRITINGS
FROM THE
ME TOO
MOVEMENT

Edited by

SHELLY ORIA

McSWEENEY'S
SAN FRANCISCO

FOREWORD

BY SHELLY ORIA

YOU KNOW THE BEGINNING: In October 2017, a major newspaper broke a story about a famous producer—a serial predator, a man who wears his ugly on his skin—and our communal ether filled with women's voices sharing private horrors, amplifying and echoing one another's words, all stamped with a hashtag. I'd recently finished writing a short story about a woman who murders men, a tale about the potential consequences of sexual harassment, and I emailed Kristina Kearns, then Executive Director of McSweeney's, asking if she'd like to publish it. I used the words *quick* and *soon*. I used the word *timeliness*. I thought: how many news cycles do we have left? I assumed that in a week the hashtag would stop trending and the world would resume its collective disinterest in everything it revealed. I spent those early days of #MeToo feeling devastated in advance.

Sometimes I laugh at my 2017 self for her fear. Here we are two years later and that news cycle still hasn't ended; it birthed a global movement. But most of the time I'm still scared—that we'll stop trying to change the reality we exposed, or that we'll keep trying and ultimately fail. That our country will keep electing Presidents and confirming Supreme Court Judges who have abused women.

My email to Kristina initiated a long exchange between us about the role art and literature should play in a crucial cultural moment. What is the point of being a publisher or editor, Kristina asked me, if one isn't responding to—and deepening—the conversation? We need a book, she said. When she asked me to be the editor, I could not have been more thrilled.

Books invite concentrated focus and offer an immersive experience. Kristina and I both felt that giving physical form to a revolution that lived predominantly on the internet would be a meaningful act.

At that time, the end of 2017, the stories of beautiful actresses, most of whom were white and straight, dominated the forming narrative (even though a black woman, Tarana Burke, founded the #MeToo movement in 2006). It felt essential to me—as a queer woman, as a writer who immigrated to this country at age twenty-five, and also as a person aware of her own privilege—to start the work of compiling this book by reaching out to writers of various backgrounds. I wanted to hear from black writers, Latinx writers, Asian writers. I wanted to hear from writers who identify as queer and writers who identify as trans. I also wanted to hear from writers who were adults before I was born, who could offer a broader perspective.

Which is to say that I wanted these sentences from contributor Honor Moore: "I remember the beginning of Women's Liberation. I don't remember particular conversations, but I remember the feeling I got when a woman declared she didn't need any movement." And this one, from contributor Gabrielle Bellot: "I had read too many stories of trans women who went to the police after men harassed them and were told by the cops that it was their own fault; what do you expect, the officers asked, when you dress like a woman?" And this one, from contributor Syreeta McFadden: "I know to expect the requisite bull-shit that comes with being a black woman in the world. I know wrong is not my name."

I wanted all these words before they were written, before they landed on the pages of this anthology. So I emailed writers and artists, people whose work had made me gasp in the past. I asked how they were doing, and I asked if they'd be willing to write about how they were doing, or if perhaps they already had. And in my email I said: give me essays, stories, poems, anything. It felt imperative to not limit the scope of this book to one genre. When collective pain and trauma yield art, our job as a society is to receive that art in all the forms it takes, in all its different garbs.

In September 2018, as I assembled these artistic testimonies, Dr. Christine Blasey Ford took the stand and shared the details of her trauma with the world. "Indelible in the hippocampus is the laughter," she said of the men who victimized her. That one of those men was subsequently confirmed as a judge on the highest court in our land is proof like no other that, to borrow Quito Ziegler's words from these pages, "we're at the early stages of a reckoning." Our fight has only just begun.

Unlike the narrator of my short story, I do not conceptualize our current reality as a gender-war. The fight, it seems to me, is one where ethical people of all genders work together paving a path toward legal and institutional change. But the act—the activism—of telling our stories started this movement and remains at its core.

Contributor Karissa Chen writes: "And now I will wait to see if telling this story, if putting it into words made permanent by ink and paper, will help exorcise the symptoms rushing through my body. I will wait to see if this is how we begin to heal our bodies, by airing out what we have forced them to reckon with silently, protectively, alone."

Let us not be alone. Let us encourage everyone's voice and act as vigilant witnesses. Let us hold one another through the aftermath of telling our stories.

YOUR STORY IS YOURS

BY KAITLYN GREENIDGE

THIS MOMENT FEELS WEIRDLY familiar. Maybe it's just that the early 1990s was when I entered therapy, but the discourse around #MeToo echoes, for me, the time when childhood sexual abuse and assault were first discussed openly. Back then, without social media, the public discussion for most women took place on daytime talk shows— Oprah Winfrey in particular will always be a hero to me for her willingness to invite survivors of sexual assault to speak on her stage. Often, it was from sources like these that those not lucky enough to encounter competent mental health professionals found the language to describe what had happened to them. It was there that an entire generation discovered the power of telling their story.

Around that time, I remember going to Boston Common to attend a rally for assault survivors. The event organizers encouraged us to write about our experiences in puffy paint on plain white T-shirts. Before social media public art demonstrations like this were a way to share these stories. I remember the profound discomfort I felt, tube of dark green fabric paint in my hand, wondering how, exactly, to make my story fit on the front of a ladies' white cotton t-shirt.

Telling your story is a key component of recovery. When you experience trauma, Broca's area—one of the parts of the brain responsible for speech and language—goes offline. It's similar to what happens when the body experiences a stroke. "Even years later, traumatized people have enormous difficulty telling other people what has happened to them," writes trauma specialist Bessel van der Kolk in *The Body Keeps the Score*. "Trauma by nature drives us to the edge of comprehension, cutting us off from language based on common experience or an imagined past." This is not to say we can't talk about it; eventually most survivors develop an explanation that they feel suits their behavior for public consumption. "These stories, however, rarely capture the inner truth of the experience," writes van der Kolk. "It is enormously difficult to organize one's traumatic experiences into a coherent account—a narrative with a beginning, a middle, and an end."

At the rally, the women and girls around me seemed to have no trouble putting their stories on their shirts, so I took a deep breath and pushed myself to write my story. A few hours later I heard a male passerby loudly reading the words on each T-shirt—including my own—to a friend walking beside him. He read with a sympathetic curiosity. Sometimes he even said, "Wow, that makes you think." But everything he said still felt awful.

If I could go back in time and speak to that girl looking skeptically at a T-shirt, I think I would say something like this:

You used to tell the story as a joke. It was easier that way. You used it as a test: you made friends with the people who laughed back. A little later, you figured out that it's best to befriend the people who grimace, then laugh. They're the ones who get it, because something similar has probably happened to them.

You will learn that the people to avoid are the ones who ask too many questions. *And then what? But where are they now? What did you do?* The questions these people ask after you tell your story are rarely about learning more information. They are not asking to better understand you, but to reassure themselves. They are making a choose-your-own-adventure story out of one of the worst things that ever happened to you. They are insisting, implicitly, that they would have done better.

Then there are the people who have had the good luck in life to find what you're describing incomprehensible. *I can't imagine. I never thought anyone could do something like that.* As they go into rhapsodies over their own innocence and naiveté, you're still there, with your story, unsure whether you want to keep telling it.

You thought you had to tell it all the time. To explain why you couldn't concentrate in class, why you couldn't keep a clean house or a man, why you sometimes looked at the buildings around you and imagined putting a match to each and every one and watching them burn.

You rationed out who knew and who didn't. When someone hurt you, in a big way or a small way, you sometimes thought, *if only they knew. If only they knew, but they don't, and they treat me like this.* There are so many stories about how the suffering of women makes them pure. You imagined, maybe, that your story would be one of those. You wrapped yourself up in that righteousness. It was warm. Almost as warm as the touch of another person.

And then, thanks to the wonder of good, competent therapy—thanks to a therapist with an understanding of generational trauma, racial trauma, poverty PTSD—you will experience a revelation: the discovery of your story's purpose. It is not a litmus test. It is not proof of emotional purity. It is not something to be measured against the pain of others. It is not there for the tortured calculations in your head of who had it worse, you or her, the woman who whispers her own story to you, who emails it to you late at night, who laughs about it with you at the bar.

As you get even older, you will learn that no one is entitled to your story. You can tell it or not tell it. People who are trying to build a philosophical argument are not entitled to your story. People who say ignorant things on the internet are not entitled to your story. People who are trying to write a novel about sexual trauma—because it's, like, so fascinating, and maybe could you give some notes—are not entitled to your story. People who do not care about your personal or emotional safety are not entitled to your story.

Your story is yours. And you get to decide how to tell it.

BYE, BABY

BY MELISSA FEBOS

KIMMY'S HOUSE IS FILLED with men. Her fridge is full
of popsicles and orange cheese. There are scratchy yellow
curtains and a bathroom too narrow for two bodies. I'm
never sure how many brothers there are, or brothers'
friends. I spend at least one night of every weekend during
sixth grade at Kimmy's house. Every week it is a battle.

"There's no supervision!" my mother yells. "You're only

twelve years old!" Kimmy's mother has the name of a boxer, or a gangster in a black-and-white movie: Pinky. After their brief phone conversations, my mother is not comforted, only exhausted enough to cave.

Kimmy's oldest brother is a football hero at the high school. He irons his T-shirts every morning and never brings his girlfriend home. It is the first real hot day of summer and we are watching him and his friends play basketball in Kimmy's driveway. There is Ty, a pretty-faced kid with tennis-ball biceps, and three of Kimmy's brothers. It is at least ninety degrees. My hair is stuck to the back of my neck with sweat and the cars are too hot to lean against. Down the potholed street a mirage shimmers, a puddle of heat.

They are huge, these boys. They smell like Old Spice and menthol cigarettes. There is anger pushing up inside them. I can hear it in their clipped voices, feel it in the sharpness of their gaze. Their bodies, even in graceful motion, are always fighting. Their limbs swing and fly, threads of sweat tumbling off them. They are louder when we watch, push each other harder, show off. Watching them, I shimmer like that mirage at the end of the street.

After a while, an older man named Vega comes around

looking for Pinky. When one of the boys yells Vega's name, I lurch in recognition. It is the name of my favorite star. When I was a child, my sea captain father would lift me up to the sky and teach me their names. He would tuck his hands under my arms, his voice beside my ear, breathing their strange sounds into the dark. *Sirius, Polaris, Arcturus, Vega.* In summer, Vega could always be found above the top of our street, flickering its changing colors. That was its atmosphere shifting, my father told me. It was bigger than my brain could hold and still it was always becoming, second by second, a different kind of beautiful.

This Vega in Kimmy's driveway is kind of beautiful, too, with his tiny moustache and golden arms. He is, in the way of men and space, both unfathomable and familiar.

Kimmy is bored. She wants to go to the mall and get an Icee. She wants to steal a bathing suit from TJ Maxx and go to the beach. She is yelling at one of the twins as her oldest brother points at me and winks.

"This one's for you," he says, and weaves his way through the grunting clot of bodies to sink the ball through the hoop. Kimmy screams. Everyone freezes, then runs to her. She has fallen on a tree branch and a piece of wood the thickness of a finger has lodged itself in her shin. It barely bleeds, the nugget of wood like a cork in her flesh. She wails, suddenly a child. Her brother carries her into a car and someone drives them to the hospital. I am left behind.

After Kimmy and her brother are gone, the rest pile into the house to raid Pinky's fridge. I follow, but stop in the living room and sit on the couch. On the mute TV screen, a girl in a miniskirt talks on a phone to a man sitting across from her, a plate of glass between them. I hear scuffles and burps from the kitchen, a bray of laughter. Ty walks out of the kitchen.

"We're going to my house," he says. My stomach twists. "You coming?" His friends titter behind him.

"C'mon man, let's go. Let the little girl alone."

"I'm not bothering her, am I?"

I shake my head.

"So, you coming?"

I tell him I'd better wait for Kimmy. He tells me I'm a good friend. I know I'm not, but I smile anyway.

"Bye, baby," he says.

Vega lingers as they leave.

"I've got to get some Odor-Eaters, bro, I've got to wait for Pinky."

"Odor-Eaters? Whatever, man, take a shower." They wave him off and get into the car outside. He watches them drive away, jingling the change in his pocket. He turns to me.

"You need anything, Mamacita? At the store, when I get my Odor-Eaters?"

I flip through channels while he's gone, turn the sound on. I go into the kitchen, with its avocado-green fridge. I take a sip of fruit punch from the plastic jug inside and wish it was grape-flavored. I love Kimmy's house despite searing moments of homesickness. During these months when my father is at sea, I sometimes can't bear to think of my mother alone, steeping in the quiet of our house.

"You want a beer?" Vega asks me when he gets back. He carries two out of the kitchen. Milwaukee's Best. I set mine down on the carpet by my foot. I have only ever tasted the foam from my father's occasional Dos Equis. Vega sits next to me on the couch. MTV is on, a man and a woman rolling around on the beach, sand stuck to their faces. The man looks at us over the woman's shoulder, squinting as he croons. The couch is too deep to lean back, so I perch on the edge.

Vega takes a long drink from his can, then balances it on the arm of the couch. He leans over and digs in the plastic bag between his feet. I can see the muscles of his back shifting through his white T-shirt. It's new; I can make out the creases from its fold inside the plastic package it came in. A black tattoo creeps out of the sleeve and down his arm. A cross, maybe. He is handsome, with sharp features and long eyelashes, but at least thirty, a grown man.

"Uh-huh," he says, and pulls a long box out of the bag and turns to me. "Odor-Eaters."

I nod. "You have stinky feet?"

"Yeah mama, I got some stinky feet."

"I can't smell them."

"That's good for you, girl." He rips open the box and pulls out a long insole. "They didn't have the powder, so I got these. Even better, right?"

I nod and frown in agreement.

He leaves the room to look for scissors.

On the TV a woman stands beside a poster of a fatter version of herself. She kicks the picture away from her and marches toward me, holding her arms out to display her new skinny body.

"Aha!" comes a muffled yell from one of the bedrooms.

Vega returns, brandishing a tiny pair of scissors with purple handles. "I found them in the twins' room." He grins at me.

I smile back.

He begins to trim the insole with the scissors. Shreds of foam snow between his knees, onto the carpet. "So, you got a boyfriend?"

"No," I say. There have been a few boys who called themselves my boyfriend. There was one I only spoke to on the phone, one who gave me a Claddagh ring with a tiny black heart clasped in gold hands.

"Oh yeah?" says Vega. "You ever date a Puerto Rican boy?"

No, I tell him, but my dad is Puerto Rican.

"Oh yeah?" he says. "So you *are* a little mamacita, huh?"

When I walk across the room toward the bathroom, my sneakers sink into the carpet like it's sand. I close the door but the lock is broken. I pee, running the faucet to hide the sound. When I'm done, I lean in to inspect my face in the medicine-cabinet mirror.

When the door opens, I am surprised and not surprised at the same time. He slides his body into the narrow space behind me. I hunch forward, as if to let him pass.

He doesn't pass. My hips press against the sink. Afraid to see his face in the mirror, I look down at the shape of my breasts under my T-shirt. I can feel the outline of his body in the aura of its warmth. Its heat is an image reflected on me. My body could wither in an instant, extinguished, a streak of smoke in the air.

He kisses the side of my neck. He breathes against my hair, my ear, my neck, and puts his hands on my waist. His index fingers press into the bare skin above the belt of my jeans. My breath comes shallow, like it does when I am afraid. I am afraid. The empty house around us feels suddenly vast, as if we were in the center of the sky or at the bottom of a hole. Vega's stubbly cheek grazes the back of my neck, and his hands slide upward. His touch is both immediate and distant: a planetary movement, a relocation of heat, light, and gravity.

A car door thunks outside. I raise my eyes, meeting his in the mirror. It feels like bursting up out of water, into light. I can move suddenly and I do, clasping my chest. I feel his fingers shift beneath my hands, and even with the fabric of my shirt between us, his hands feel as if they are inside of me, a part of my own body. I know I will never tell anyone about this. Voices in the driveway grow louder, then spill into the house through an opened door. Vega's hands slide down my belly. He leans back against the wall and I push the door open and rush into the hall, where Kimmy and her brothers wait.

HOW DID IT ALL BEGIN?

BY SYREETA McFADDEN

"BUT HOW DID IT all begin?" writes Roberto Calasso in *The Marriage of Cadmus and Harmony*. He repeats this question in his whimsical retelling of the story of Zeus luring the maiden Europa away across unknown waters, disguised as a white bull. Calasso is assigned reading for a seminar that I'm a student in Bronxville in 2006, a rigorous academic interrogation of gender in world myths. Calasso's rendering makes the story beautiful, his language dream-like and ephemeral and present:

Europa, meantime, could see no end to this crazy sea crossing. But she guessed what would happen to her when they hit land again. And she shouted to the wind and water: "Tell my father Europa has been carried off by a bull—my kidnapper, my sailor, my future bedmate, I imagine."

My kidnapper, my sailor, my future bedmate, I imagine. This is the first time I've read a version where Europa speaks. The prose is as plaintive as it is poetic: a woman slowly realizing her future rape, resigning herself to the fact that this is how it is and always will be. How appropriate that the language of this story captures the predator-prey binary we have always used to define male and female sexuality.

"There were plenty of witnesses," Calasso continues. Consent apparently didn't exist in antiquity, but complicity is as old as dirt. And here it hit me: the origin story of the continent itself is a story of rape masquerading as male eroticism.

Not much later, a woman in my fiction seminar shares a haunting recurring dream of a bull, deep in the darkness of an unnamed ocean, marching. It has taken her body, she feels, to some unknown place. She is white, and as she talks she grows pale. I wonder, from where I sit, whether you truly can smell fear. If you can, hers smells like damp cement and copper. She speaks as if it were larger than a recurring dream, a thing actually happening to her in her waking life. As if she can still see the dull eyes of a bull in the blue-black dark of the ocean floor.

"But how did it all begin?" they ask.

Today the electricians and I are discussing the American Civil War and slavery. I am their teacher: teaching language, literature, history, politics. I'm teaching them humanity and, subversively, feminism, without ever uttering the word itself. I am a black woman, which comes with its own set of misconceptions.

Their memory of U.S. history is spotty, and they dig for specifics. Mostly they repeat the stories they were told about the South. I do not sugarcoat the fact that American capital was built on enslaved African labor. I ask them to think critically about the importation of enslaved Africans. I note that the importation of slave labor in the U.S. ended in 1807, when the population of enslaved Africans was slightly over one million. I add that, prior to the start of the Civil War, that number was more than 4 million. They look puzzled. I ask them to do the math. I tell them the values of enslaved children and persons by age and gender, placing particular emphasis on the fact that children and young women of childbearing age yielded a higher value than men. A slow realization crystallizes in their eyes before I even have to say it.

"You mean, they weren't using sex to advance their position?" one electrician asks.

"Have you considered that it wasn't even a choice?" I ask.

"who in the hell set things up / like this," June Jordan asks, and later answers, in "A Poem About My Rights." Jordan's poem first appeared in *Essence* in 1978, and her rage is still palpable. It articulates and contextualizes our collective and sustained fury better than I can today.

> *"I have been the meaning of rape*
> *I have been the problem*
> *everyone seeks to eliminate by forced*

penetration with or without the evidence of slime and
but let this be unmistakable this poem
is not consent I do not consent..."

It is December in the year of our great reckoning, the year when hundreds, perhaps thousands, of stories of assault, harassment, and rape of women by powerful (and not so powerful) men have finally been revealed, when I find myself alone in a theater, watching a documentary about Recy Taylor. Taylor, a twenty-four-year-old black woman in Abbeville, Alabama, was the victim of a brutal rape at gunpoint by four white teenage boys in 1944, and she did the unthinkable after surviving such an ordeal: she told her story. Listening to her tell it, I reach for lines from Jordan's poem. I loop on "I am not wrong / wrong is not my name." I learn something I had failed to consider: it was common practice for Southern white men to abduct black women from backwoods country roads—when they were alone after their shifts cleaning those men's homes, starching their oxfords, feeding their children—to assault and rape them.

The story of black migration to northern cities centers on the persecution of black men, falsely accused of raping white women and later lynched for these imagined crimes. It never occurred to me that sexual assault of black women by white men was so epidemic that we should have expected a flight to the north.

In her book *Sister Citizen,* Melissa Harris-Perry describes the "misrecognition" of black women in American society, explicitly noting that the Victorian ideals of feminine identity were never assigned to black women. Moreover, these ideals established myths about the wantonness and licentiousness and hypersexualization of black women. Black women were not to be afforded protection or humanity. They were unwomen. This was cover for white men to rape them with impunity. This is how the social order was upheld by slave societies and extended through Jim Crow, continuous rape of black women and all.

My grandmothers and great-aunts never discussed these things.

The dreams that terrify me most are the ones in which I cannot scream.

One time, a man in a crowded bar stopped me, exchanged a set of odd words with me. Amused, I humored him. I don't remember how it happened, but before I could walk away, he kissed me.

While I didn't resist, I froze. Only today do I recognize it as a post-traumatic response. In that moment, I did feel some shame about my delay in fighting back. I left my body. Yet I also understood that my doing so was equal parts examining the fantasy projected onto me and coddling him for both my safety and his. We were both black in a bar in New York City, surrounded by mostly white people. I did not consent to this kiss, but I feared for him. He seemed to be immersed in his own narrative, some kind of fairy tale, an invention about courtship. Perhaps he imagined himself as a beguiling, charming apparition—a white bull—and naturally, as a woman but even more like an object, I'd yield and recognize him as a romantic other. What I do know is that I sensed danger, sensed how quickly this mirage of romance could turn toxic, vitriolic, and violent.

My delay in fighting back and rejecting him likely taught him two things about women, notably black women, as a black man. I didn't want to seem unkind.

* * *

The curator's notes for Jean-Francois de Troy's painting *The Abduction of Europa*, at the National Gallery in Washington, D.C., describes it as "delightful." The painting is washed in bright colors, soft pastels dappled with rich reds and blues. The bull is a brilliant white. The brushstrokes are fluid, bulbous, and soft. Europa's body is contorted in a way that communicates a kind of rapture, of being swept up in a moment. A reckoning, maybe. The curator notes that this story has "captured the imagination of European artists for centuries." These artists were all male. Strip away any critical thinking about what the images and myths are telling you and you might indeed consider the painting delightful.

What I remember most about the moment is simply the dark.

I remember being told one thing that led me there and how slowly I came to realize it was a lie. I remember cold concrete on my bare back, a summer girlchild dress pushed upward. My mind reels and I remember being pulled from a hotel poolside into the deep end many years later. I remember sinking. I remember my fight back and I pulled myself from the darkest poolside blue. I don't remember a bull. I don't remember his face. I do know I screamed *Stop*. I must have drawn blood, pulled his skin, trapped some of it between my nails. I do not know how all of this began. Or who set things up like this. Or why we believed this is how it always is. I remember freezing when he came up behind me in the backyard. Or was it a bar? Or a crowded banquet hall? I was thirty years old. I think he was an ox. It doesn't matter what I wore. I have a curvy backside. I might even be considered beautiful. I know to expect the requisite bullshit that comes with being a black woman in the world. I know wrong is not my name.

THE WOMEN'S MARCH

BY REBECCA SCHIFF

SHE DIDN'T GO TO the Women's March. She didn't write "me too." She still belonged to at least twelve women-only literary groups, but she'd turned off notifications, hidden them all. In the shower she scrubbed her vagina and said "fuck this." The women-only health group said not to use soap. The women-only health group had more than nine thousand members and a trigger warning on every post. Her nipple had a pimple. Was it a literary pimple? She squeezed for pus and blood.

As a virgin, she'd marched for choice. She'd escorted poor women past other screaming poor people at a clinic in Bridgeport, Connecticut. Eighty dicks later, no pregnancies, she stayed home, updating her Facebook preferences. She drank a women's tea. The teabag said beauty came from helping others find their strength.

Her phone rang for the first time in eight days. It was her friend calling to talk about rape. Neither of them had been raped, though they'd collectively had their crotch grabbed in Italy and been masturbated at in an elevator in the Bronx. That was it, not bad. Her friend had ridden around in a police car looking for the masturbator.

All her dicks had been consensual, except one she stopped in the middle. He threw the condom in her plant. He later emailed "not my finest hour." He was Churchillian, if Churchill had been a Jewish painter who painted ugly rainbows. She'd also had a stalker in college, but when she told him to stop stalking her, he stopped. Where was he now? Had he married? Did he still write poetry? She stalked her stalker.

She'd been lucky in rape, unlucky in other ways. She was counting on luck to keep her rapeless, counting on street greetings to stay greetings. "Hi," she said. "Good evening." The formality was protection. Bigger people told her to learn jujitsu. Her dates tried to walk her home, but a "this is me" at the corner meant she'd risk the last half block without them.

Who was she? She was a woman and she was a corner. She tried to take up knitting. She used pens from La Quinta Inn. Nobody had forced himself into her, not once, and if anybody ever tried she had no plan except to scream, which was everybody's plan, except maybe women who'd taken self-defense. So she should sign up, but she won't sign up. She'll fake-knit for a week and then give the yarn to a friend who really knits. She'll write with hotel pens, be bossed around by tea, make up new chants in the shower. "We're women, we measure, we're not here for your pleasure!" She'll keep this to herself, her gift for making dumb things rhyme.

EVOLUTIONARY THEORY

BY DIANA SPECHLER

"Nor could we check our sympathy,
even at the urging of hard reason...."

> —Charles Darwin, *The Descent of Man, and
> Selection in Relation to Sex*

I.

I WAS A COCKTAIL WAITRESS carrying a tray of glasses above my head. I passed a man in a loosened necktie who tickled my bare armpit.

What did she do?

I kept walking. I set the glasses down in the kitchen. I took a deep breath, the way they suggest. And then I returned to the bar.

Were the glasses empty or full?

Some contained melting ice, others were half-empty, one housed a chewed straw and a squished wedge of lemon.

Why was her armpit bare?

I was wearing a tank top.

Why had she worn a tank top to work?

It was early 2009. Business was slow. A customer had recently given me a Bear Stearns pen and suggested I sell it on eBay in twenty years. The tank top in question was the one I called my "recession shirt." It was a little bit see-through.

Where is the pen now?

I don't know.

Why is she careless with the gifts of men?

I have trouble discerning which ones are gifts.

Why didn't she grab the fellow by the scruff and give him a what-for? My mother sure would have. Woe to any tickler who lays a finger on my mother.

I was carrying a full tray over my head.

But what about later? Why are we hearing only now

about an incident from 2009 that was not even sexual, seeing as no genitals were involved?

I felt bad for the man in the loosened tie. His lips were stained by Red Bull. He looked like a little boy.

2.

I was a waitress in a movie theater in Texas. My uniform was all black; we were supposed to be invisible. My boss, Chad, who had previously managed a Planet Hollywood, stopped me in the corridor behind the theaters and laughed. He said, "I almost just said to you, 'Wanna fuck?'" Then he chuckled a little more and kept walking.

Did she react to what he didn't say?

I told his boss.

She ratted him out?

I felt that reporting him was the right thing to do.

Was it the right thing to do?

No.

Why not?

Because Chad's boss told Chad, who made me work *What Lies Beneath* over and over and over again. No one wanted to work that cheap-thrills horror flick in which

Michelle Pfeiffer's husband tries to drown her in a bathtub. If you delivered a burger during *What Lies Beneath*, the customer would startle and scream or fall out of her seat. Also he kept telling me to put my hair in a ponytail.

Why wasn't her hair in a ponytail?

I'd been having headaches.

Why didn't she do something?

I did.

But something with a little oomph.

It was Darwin who said, "The male sex is universally preferred to the female."

He was a wonderful observer. Dare I say our sharpest.

I felt overwhelming sadness when Chad talked about his Planet Hollywood days. He loved Planet Hollywood. Sometimes he still wore the cap.

3.

Do you know that if you google "famous evolutionary biologists," you'll see the faces of ten white men?

She sounds like a schoolmarm.

Sorry.

Like a moralistic shrew.

Sorry.

Those are men from a glorious time. We owe so much to that time and those men.

4.

I was broke in 2006. I had just moved to New York and was waitressing in both a bar and a restaurant. There was never enough money. Two men in the span of three months presented me with solutions. One was a self-published author of "history books." We gave a reading together in the East Village and then he kept sending me emails and showing up at the bar. After I spilled Thai soup on my laptop, he said he would buy me a new one in exchange for "the pleasure" of my "company." The second man was my boss at the restaurant. He offered me an apartment to live in rent-free if I would regularly have sex with him in it.

Did she agree to either deal?

No.

Did she report her boss?

No.

Did she seek alternative employment opportunities?

No.

She continued to work for a man whom she now claims is a predator.

Yes.

She endangered other women.

Probably.

Yet she calls herself a victim.

I do not call myself a victim.

Does she expect sympathy for these alleged events, more than a decade later?

No.

Did she consider agreeing to either deal?

Both.

What stopped her?

The stigma against sex workers, what I imagined their penises looked like, the word *ruined*, the pepper spray my grandfather had sent me in the mail, an old home movie in which I'm preverbal and petting a goat.

What did she tell the generous author?

That I distrust men who give me things more than I distrust men who ask me for things.

Did she take pride in that turn of phrase?

Yes.

Did he appreciate her purported eloquence?
He told me I was plain-looking.
Now we're getting to the source of the anger.
Or maybe he said "just normal-looking."
How did she respond to her boss's flirtation?
I laughed.
She laughed.
We often laugh. And thereby preserve the species.

5.

I was a waitress at a bar in Boulder, Colorado. A customer in a Hawaiian shirt who looked twice my age followed me to the computer where I was placing his order. He told me he was going to change my life. He was a famous rock climber who was making a movie about rock climbing. He asked me if I wanted to be a travel writer.

Did she want to be a travel writer?

I wanted to be a poet. I was writing a lot of poems that summer, and being treated for an eating disorder, and I was in love with the bartender at work who wore a house-arrest ankle bracelet and wouldn't love me back. The next day, the rock climber called the bar looking for me. I returned his call at the bartender's urging. The bartender admired the rock climber. He loved to climb rocks when he wasn't under house arrest.

What happened when she placed the call?

The rock climber told me to send him a writing sample.

Did she have a writing sample to send him?

I had my college honors thesis, a collection of experimental short stories called *The Asymmetry of Heat.*

LOL.

Sorry.

Did he find the stories promising?

He said they confirmed what he'd already sensed: that there was "something special" about me. He decided to take me out for sushi so we could discuss my future.

Please list the expectations she pinned to that dinner.

That I would magically become a travel writer. That the bartender would fall in love with me. That I would circumvent pain, such as working toward a life as an artist, such as aging, such as weight gain, such as death (others' and mine).

Did the rock climber fulfill her expectations?

The rock climber stared at my breasts. Then he took me to a bookstore and bought me his own book, a memoir about rock climbing that featured his image on the cover. Then I went home and binged on a box of chocolate calcium chews, which resulted in four hours of diarrhea.

Was she wearing the see-through tank top?

I did not yet own the see-through tank top.

"Look up here, Buster," my mother would have said. "My eyes are up here on my face!"

That's a good one.

And now... how many years later?

Seventeen.

Seventeen! Now she wants to blame this minor celebrity whose only crimes are scaling mountains and putting his heart on the line?

It takes many years for a woman to blame a man.

Is she quoting Darwin?

I am summarizing history.

Who paid for dinner?

The rock climber.

Who paid for the sake?

The rock climber.

Who left the tip?

The rock climber.

What became of the bartender?

I went home with him after work the next night. In the morning he told me he didn't want a girlfriend.

Can we assume that she immediately vacated the premises?

I cried so hard I couldn't speak. Then when I could speak, I told him I had an eating disorder. He looked like he didn't know what to do. He rubbed his face with both hands. Then he asked me if I wanted to meet his friend's puppies.

Did she meet the puppies?

I sat on the bartender's lawn with him. He couldn't go anywhere because of the house arrest. We didn't say much. The bartender was going through hard times, too. His father had recently died. The bartender had a problem with alcohol and another with rage. I think he loved me in a way, the way you love young, sad people when you are young and sad.

She has not answered the question.

His friend arrived with the puppies. The friend was a girl, probably one he was sleeping with. I remember she was from Arkansas and all the boys called her Arkansas. She looked momentarily confused when she saw me, as if she'd caught her own reflection without warning. There was a lot of sun in the sky that day and the puppies were warm and they smelled like the earth. I put one against my neck.

She accepted her role as nurturer.

I wanted to explain something to Arkansas, but I figured she already knew. The bartender was running in circles, letting a puppy chase him. I was thinking about his father. I was missing his father for him. I was wondering if his father was the reason he couldn't love me, or if I was the reason.

Is it fair to say that she felt better?

I was happy that the puppy was giving him so much love.

Is it fair to say that she—

Yes. I think he felt better.

A PROMISE OBTAINED BY COERCION IS NEVER BINDING

BY HOSSANNAH ASUNCION

IN ONE EAR,
the languid violin,
in the other,
the language of violence.
Breathe into the fold—
can you whisper crush me,
speak a gentle weep,
follow the cut,
salve before scar.
Bring flowers.
Bring candy.

DEARBORN
STREET

BY NELLY REIFLER

ALBION STREET. DEARBORN STREET. Linda Street. Lapidge Street. These are the alleys that run north and south between Valencia and Guerrero, from 16th Street to the dead end near 20th. Each neighborhood in San Francisco has its own climate. After the fog rolls into areas close to the Pacific, for instance, you find yourself under a roiling, soggy sky. But in the Mission, the sky becomes silver-white and flat, like a nickel pressing low on the grid.

Many days, I walked these Mission alleys. I felt cozy in the narrow passages, like a small animal. I daydreamed while I walked. I was twenty-four.

If you are a woman, you have been followed. If you are a girl, you have been followed. If you have not been followed, you will be soon. You may hear a sound first: breath, footfall, cloth on cloth. Or you may see something from the corner of your eye: a quick flash of flesh or hair, the bill of a cap worn low. Or you may simply *feel* it: a change in the air currents, the humidity of another's breath, the sense of a human presence pacing itself with your pace or getting nearer.

I felt him there, close behind me, slightly to the left. I felt the way his feet stayed near the ground as he stepped. He had been following me since 16th Street. We walked, almost together, down Albion Street, past orange and red poppies in a window box, past graffiti and a powder-blue convertible. He was silent. I hooked right on 17th. I did not head down to Valencia, that wide open boulevard. I was stubborn. You are not being followed, I told myself. If a man is walking in the same direction you are walking, and he happens to be walking behind you, that does not mean he is following you. It merely means he needs to travel by foot from north to south.

From 17th Street I turned onto Dearborn. The man turned, too, and as he did, I glimpsed his brown suit, his white cuffs, his shiny black shoes, his balding head.

I began to walk faster. So did he. Then he was at my shoulder.

"Girl," he said. "Hello, girl."

You are not being followed, I told myself. "Hello," I said, and walked faster.

"Girl. Little girl."

I walked past stoops and vinyl siding and an empty parked van. He walked faster, past stoops and vinyl siding and an empty parked van. He walked at my side. His hot breath fogged my neck and ear.

"Girl, you are a little girl. My car is up the street, girl."

My own breaths were shallow. I felt them catch in my throat. Inhaling was almost impossible. I tried to walk faster. I could not.

"My car is up the street," he said again. "And you're so

little, I could pick you up and put you in my suitcase, and put my suitcase in my trunk, and drive you to my hotel."

I didn't run.

"I could drive you to my hotel. I could take you to my room."

I reached the end of Dearborn Street. I hesitated. I looked west, then east.

The man and his brown suit and bald head were on me.

He didn't say anything. He didn't have to. I was so small, he could put me in his suitcase, put his suitcase in his trunk, and drive me to his hotel and take me to his room.

I turned and ran down 18th Street to Valencia, wide and bare and empty of people. The white sun beat down. I stood on the corner and panted. I thought I had lost him. Then he appeared again.

He took me, easily, and dragged me, easily, and pushed me, easily, into a recessed garage door. He pressed himself into me. The whole weight of him pressed my back into the door's metal ridges. I smelled his sweat and sebum. I felt his steam.

Small animals are easy to grab and carry, but they can also slip out from a predator's grasp.

I buckled my knees and ducked under his arm and slid

out from under his weight. Again I ran, this time to the deli across the street. I could see him watching and waiting. I used the store's phone and called my boyfriend, who came and picked me up.

We bought falafel at the deli and walked to Linda Street. A kid dribbled a basketball on the court across the way. The dealer with his dime bags sat on our stoop. The stairwell smelled like enamel paint. In our apartment, we ate the falafel. I couldn't say what had happened. I couldn't describe the man. We talked about our jobs, and we kissed, and we went to sleep on our mattress by the window.

I'm so small I can fit in your suitcase. You can put me in your suitcase and in the trunk of your car. You can drive me to your hotel and take me to your room. You can. I know.

HOT FOR TEACHER

BY COURTNEY ZOFFNESS

WHAT DID THEY WANT? More than anything? Violent things. Unattainable things.

More than anything, she wanted to taste blood, said one student.

More than anything, he wanted freedom, said another.

Your characters need to have desires, I'd explained in the previous class. Drama arises when people struggle to get what they want.

Their first writing assignment of the semester at this midsize East Coast college: compose a short fictional sketch that begins with wanting. Compelling, complex fiction, I'd said, grows out of desires great and small. Their opening sentences offered proof.

More than anything, she wanted a baby.

More than anything, he wanted things to return to the way they were.

Then we arrived at Charlie in the back row, a pale, acne-pocked sophomore who rarely participated in class discussions. I'd surmised he was shy, but it was early in the term. I was making assumptions.

More than anything, Charlie read in an even voice, he wanted for her to realize that she shouldn't depend on the bankers or lawyers she probably dated, that it wasn't them who could really and truly satisfy her, but that it was him, a student in her Tuesday writing class, him who could and would push aside the pile of ungraded papers and take her passionately atop her desk, him with whom she belonged in a way that only the romantic poetry she taught them could convey.

Twenty pairs of eyes pinned me in place. I willed my face not to blush, my voice not to crack.

Okay, I said, just as I had to the student who'd shared work before him.

More than anything, I wanted to scream expletives in his face.

Charlie's expression was inscrutable; he seemed neither proud, nor nervous. Perhaps a little expectant, like he'd just ordered take-out and was waiting to be told how much it cost. That passage, I said, has a nice rhythm to it, a nice cadence. I leaned back against the table, my rear precariously close to the pile of ungraded papers. I would not let him have his way with me. The repetition, I said, is poetic.

The repetition, I wanted to say, keeps your voice loud while mine is silent.

I moved on to the student next to him, one whose character, more than anything, wanted a piece of pie.

It is February in Brooklyn and the café speakers try to counteract the cold. They blast Southern soul in the form of Joe Tex's "I Gotcha," a song I remember from *Reservoir Dogs*. You'll recognize the story in its lyrics; it might even be yours. It was mine one Friday night in high school when I left my friend's basement to use the upstairs bathroom.

The upper floor was dark, the house asleep, but I knew the way. Afterwards, when I emerged into the shadowy hallway, her older brother's friend was waiting—for the toilet, I assumed. I recognized his football jersey and backwards baseball cap, but not the thin-lipped smile he put inches from my face, nor the pressure of his bony hands on my hips nor the way he moved his body side to side with mine as I tried to dodge him. The entrapment dance. When I retreated backwards, he stepped forward, until my heel hit the tile at the entrance to the bathroom. He was going to push me in there, I realized. He was going to push me onto the cold floor and lock the door behind him and everyone was in the basement and nobody would hear me scream. I tasted iron in the back of my throat, a bloody nose, and belted—*let me through!*—and somehow wriggled past.

But we're not talking about a dance, we're talking about a song. A groovy, horn-filled tune whose lyrics describe how a man, more than anything, wants a woman against her will.

Now, kiss me
Hold it a long time, hold it
Don't turn it a-loose, now hold it

*   *   *

My first-ever intimate encounter was an unwelcome kiss. I was nine. Todd had advertised his crush on me, told classmates I had a *nice ass*, crude language that made me giggle with embarrassment. Was I supposed to feel flattered? Miffed? (Todd would later try to retract, slipping a sheet of yellow paper into the cave of my school desk, a letter I inexplicably saved: *I'm sorry for what I said. You do have a nice ass, but only in jeans.*)

One afternoon in the park, Todd announced that he wanted a kiss. *Your characters need to have desires.* I didn't want to kiss him, nor did I want to be kissed, but the more I refused, the more he insisted, until a chase ensued. Just a kiss, he called. I sprinted and screamed: No! Everyone laughed and cheered him on, including my girlfriends. Terror bloomed in my blood. *Drama arises when people struggle to get what they want.* I wound up curled face-down in the dirt, hands and arms blocking the sides of my face, heart hammering.

What was I afraid of? I couldn't tell you then, but I can tell you now. Impotence. How words we both understood— *leave me alone!*—had no effect.

Todd found a sliver of exposed skin between my earlobe and neck and crushed his lips against it.

I was twenty-nine in that East Coast classroom, young for an academic, but not a newbie. I'd already taught hundreds of students, and several challenging charges. I had practice diverting attention away from in-class disruptions and channeling excitement into animated discussions. Still, I couldn't determine what Charlie wanted. To see me squirm? Flush? Freak out? I broke the class into groups to complete a collaborative exercise. Did he expect a sultry invitation to office hours? Or was this his idea of a joke? A performance for classmates? A way to shove the teacher while everyone watched to see if she'd wobble, then fall?

In high school, I became the fixation of a foreign-exchange student. Farouk not only memorized my schedule but seemed to know its digressions. If I showed up early to work in the painting studio, Farouk would find me and try to make small talk, apologizing for his poor English. He attended my sports matches, once lingered outside my math class—a bodiless face framed in the door's small window. I laughed off his overtures, poked fun at them with friends. I thought that ignoring him would translate my disinterest and hamper his, but he only redoubled his efforts. Farouk sent gifts to my house and oversized cards featuring black-and-white stock photos of a little boy and girl. In one, they sat on a stoop, his lips pressed to her cheek, her long-lashed eyes circular and open wide. I was his perfect girl, he wrote, amidst blobs of Wite-Out. Couldn't he be my friend?

Most of Farouk's packages included self-addressed stamped envelopes to facilitate a reply, which he never received.

I didn't seek formal intervention because his advances, while excessive, didn't seem threatening to my school-aged self. Not even when he proclaimed he'd always love me in our senior yearbook, alongside his national farewell: *See ya, USA!*

Then there's the doctor who I saw from pubescence through my early twenties. An obstetrician. He treated my mother, too. Doctor gave me breast exams with clammy pink hands, during which he engaged in small talk. Where was I applying to college? Did I know what I wanted to study? It was good I liked to read, he said, because we might be snowed in over the weekend. Had I heard about the forecasted storm? He was thorough with the palpating, he said, because I had dense breasts. Up close the hairs of his white moustache and beard were thicker than I expected, his forehead more mottled. His wedding band felt cool against my skin.

Doctor was the first man to touch me. He gave me pelvic exams and asked questions about my sexual habits and told me that the structure of my anatomy, intercourse in certain positions would be uncomfortable. He tilted his head, asked if this was the case. Was it? Uncomfortable?

Shortly thereafter, in a crowded rock club, someone slipped a hand up my skirt and fingers inside me. I shrieked and spun around, but the bass overwhelmed my voice and in the low light there was only a lattice of flesh, lips and hands shifting and slithering, one mighty, insidious beast.

*   *   *

Should I have done more to protect myself? Even as a grown woman I was steeped in self-doubt. By the end of my class with Charlie, I'd determined I needed to be more objective. This was a creative writing class, one in which we read stories across the inflammatory spectrum. Maybe I was overreacting. Maybe I misremembered the specific-ity of the student's writing, or its intensity—dismissive tendencies that, I see now, encourage rapacious behavior.

I located his assignment on the train home and discov-ered, in sentence two, that his character favored his profes-sor's striped sweater dress—something I'd worn to our last class—which highlighted her pendulous breasts. The next page offered similar drivel. I slammed my folder closed.

College: a middle-of-the-night phone call from a guy who said he got my name from a mutual friend. The caller thought I was pretty "in a natural way." He hoped we could talk. When, in a sleepy daze, I pressed—which friend again?—the line went dead. I dismissed the exchange as a prank, until he called a few nights later, and again, the night after that. Each time I slammed down the phone, and only half-remembered the occurrence the following morning. When, on his fifth or sixth call, he complimented my cute blue row house, I called the police. The officers had neither a number nor a name to trace—this was 1999—so other than showing up in the morning's wee hours to record my complaint, they could only offer words.

Be vigilant, they said. Be careful. Let us know if there's any more activity.

There was plenty of activity—for an agitated imagination. For weeks, I eyeballed every lone male in my path, analyzed every noise outside my window, and jogged to and from my evening classes with keys laced between my fingers. I struggled to sleep. Feared my ringing phone, and feared unplugging it, too.

Maybe the caller was a neighbor. Maybe he was peering out his window when the squad car pulled up, and watched me welcome officers into my cute blue row house, face warped with worry. Maybe he realized he'd gone too far. Or didn't want to get caught. He never called again.

Was it? Uncomfortable? What was uncomfortable was Doctor's question, which I assumed was par for the course in a gynecological exam. After all, I was paying a stranger to handle and inquire about my private parts. Sometimes, in his office, I'd stare at the framed photos of his blonde children to feel more at ease.

When precancerous cells were discovered on my cervix, Doctor performed the excision. I was 22. My mother joined, and I squeezed her hand while he peered between my legs and spread numbing gel on my cervix and used a hot electrical wire to cut away abnormal tissue. Afterwards, I cramped and bled.

I moved to Baltimore for graduate school a few months later, and found a new doctor.

My boyfriend, neither a lawyer nor a banker as Charlie assumed, was outraged. The kid sounds psychotic, he said. You shouldn't go back to class.

That's absurd, I replied, unwilling to cower. Of course, the thought occurred to me, too. This was months after the Virginia Tech massacre wherein a male undergrad killed thirty-two people, the deadliest mass shooting on a college campus to date. The gunman had intimidated girls in his poetry class by taking pictures of their legs. Which is not to say I thought Charlie was plotting murder. I just couldn't read his behavior.

Neither could the English department chair, to whom I forwarded his assignment. She was apprehensive when she called him in for a one-on-one meeting the following day, joking to me that if the worst-case scenario came to pass, I could have her back issues of the *Paris Review*. Charlie, meanwhile, was baffled—or acted that way. He'd not only changed the day our class met, he told her, but changed the color of my hair! As he seemed neither hostile nor deranged, and since he apologized, his sentence was reassignment. He commenced an independent study with a male professor. For the rest of the semester, I considered how it didn't matter that I had ten years on Charlie or more degrees, that I could fail him with the stroke of a pen. He still felt compelled to exert sexual power. I was still a woman.

It's a catchy tune that's filling up the café. Customers tap their feet and hum.

You made me a promise and you're gonna stick to it
You shouldn't have promised if you weren't gonna do it

Survey the crowd. There are familiar faces there: my

sons, ages four and six. They like the song, too. They bop their heads, lick whipped cream off hot chocolate.

You saw me and ran in another direction
I'll teach you to play with my affection

Later, when I hear my boys singing the chorus—*Give it here!*—I can explain that I dislike its message, that a man's Yes is never more powerful than a woman's No. I can parlay this into the Respect People's Bodies talk that some teachers have advised parents to impart. You shouldn't touch another person, and no person should touch you, without permission, I can say. Ask before you hug someone. Assert *no thank you* to the offer of a hug if you're not in the mood. Same with holding hands: ask or give permission.

I can teach them about sexism, too, point to inescapable indoctrinations: the Mrs. and Miss titles they use alongside the singular Mr.; the male faces emblazoned on coins in their piggybanks; the boy toys endorsing confrontational play. I can explain how inequality begets bias begets discrimination begets intimidation begets assault. How if they see anyone forcing a kiss upon someone, they should intervene. That allowing such behavior not only implicates them, but permits another act one degree more heinous, and makes witnesses one degree more tolerant, until there's no shame in grabbing a woman by the pussy, until 62 million Americans say Yes to a presidential candidate who brags about doing just that.

I can model good behavior, too. Can take aside that boy on the playground who's pulling a girl's hair while she squeals.

Let's not do that, I tell him. She's letting you know she doesn't like it.

The girl sniffles. The boy takes off.

Watch my sons watch me. It's good to be a helper, I say.

In 2015, a suit filed in Manhattan Supreme Court detailed Doctor's rampant sexual abuse, including how he vaginally and anally probed female patients with glove-less fingers. Nineteen women described behavior dating back to the early 1990s. Nine of them had been pregnant at the time. Oftentimes Doctor would examine women with a nurse present and then return after the nurse left, claiming he forgot to check something. At trial, he admitted to forcibly touching one woman to "gratify" his sexual desire and to engaging in "sexual conduct against a patient for no valid medical purpose while she was incapable of consent." More than one woman felt his tongue between their legs.

Due to the criminal statute of limitations for most victims, and Doctor's fierce defense, which worked to discredit accusers, Doctor landed a handsome deal: he plead guilty to one low-level felony and a misdemeanor, and instead of going to jail, he forfeited his medical license. Since the DA agreed to downgrade Doctor's sex offender status to the lowest level, he doesn't even appear on the sex offender registry.

Summer 2018. I am a faculty member in a writing program in Greece. I bring along my family and my four-year-old, Leo, strikes up a friendship with a local girl named Ivana. For days they are inseparable, playing tag, trading bites of ice cream, searching for stray cats. One evening, while they pose for photos at an adult's behest, someone shouts, Kiss her, Leo! A minor chorus erupts: kiss her, kiss her! Leo leans over, holds his pucker to Ivana's face while flashes flicker.

I could've interceded. Said, why don't they just smile? But there is live music and dancing and everyone is merry and I don't want to be a killjoy. It is over in seconds.

Ivana seems unbothered. After she leaves to play, a friend shows me his camera snapshot. In it, Leo's eyes are shut tight, Ivana's wide open.

THE GREAT TRANSITION

BY QUITO ZIEGLER

IT STARTS WHEN YOU say it in words, that first push of bravery. The shock of hearing yourself tell another human: *I was raped.*

Sometimes that silence takes years to break. Sometimes forever.

You are a survivor now. Things are going to change— you must accept that you have entered a process of transformation. It's going to take time but if you keep doing the work, you will get through it. I guarantee it.

Eventually you realize that you are not alone. People of all genders and colors have been surviving patriarchal violence in all its forms for centuries. From #MeToo to All Of Us. Our individual stories add up to a great big society in need of serious healing and transformation.

In my dreams I call it the Great Transition.

Transition starts from the idea of change and progresses on until, years later, you're living your life as the person of your dreams. Not without your struggles, but with most of the process behind you.

The public feminist awakening unfolding around us often strikes me as a scaled-up version of my gender transition from cis to nonbinary, which incidentally began when I broke my silence about sexual assault in my childhood. In my story, gender transition and healing from sexual violence became completely entwined.

Gender transition can be reduced to two distinct processes—a psychological reckoning inside of your head, and a physical transformation, involving drag, meds, hormones, appointments, paperwork, process.

To me the Great Transition is the period we are living through now, when the cracks in the structures are visible to anyone who chooses to see them. If we consider #MeToo the early stages of a much longer process, and understand it through the lessons learned from gender transition, we can see through the turbulence to the light ahead.

Right now we are feeling the pain of announcement, the shock of trauma. We are coming to terms with terrible violence on a massive scale, and it is both painful and powerful. On a timeline of transition, we're at the early stages of a reckoning.

Grief comes in stages: shock, denial, anger, bargaining, depression, acceptance. That's a lot of feelings to work through as individuals, and even more to consider as institutions, as fields, as a culture. Right now, any group of people that calls itself a community is due for a reckoning with the violence, subtle or heinous, that has been perpetuated—and overlooked, underreported, stigmatized, gaslit—for centuries.

Reckoning doesn't feel nice. It's never pretty. There are a million rabbit holes to fall down: how could this happen to us? Why is society structured to support this? Who put these rules into place? Who enforces them? Why? How long has this been going on?

But reckoning is essential for healing from trauma.

*   *   *

A moment to remember the survivors who came before, in 500 years of patriarchal rule on this land: Indigenous women, nothing like Disney's Pocahontas. Enslaved women raped by masters. Japanese women forced into camps. Wives dominated by husbands.

The gift of the #MeToo movement is that at last it sheds the light on how many of us have experienced gender-based harassment and violence. Our next steps need to acknowledge how much broader the conversation needs to be.

Once you consider all of the intersectional overlaps, all of the identities, all of the experiences, you realize how deep the problems have become, how deep the change needs to be.

Which leads us from reckoning to transformation.

*   *   *

We don't actually have time for this modern-day bullshit, for these orange-colored nightmares we keep hallucinating when we point our eyes screenward. It's preparing us for a battle, though we need to stop framing it this way because that perpetuates a language of violence. We need a shift in tone, one that filters through our structures and institutions and behaviors, right down to our very own brains.

The shift is a process too, and it won't happen without a real commitment to seeing the work through. Structural change doesn't happen overnight. Forgiveness isn't easy. The process involves showing up to do the work, repeatedly, over time: meetings, conversations, phone calls, dinners, self-care breaks, town halls. Changes. Restructuring. Transformation.

My own transformation has involved listening, listening, listening, finally changing my life to bring it closer to my values.

GLAD PAST WORDS

BY MECCA JAMILAH SULLIVAN

FOR A WHILE, SHANIECE Armistice Guzmán tried to
convince herself nothing had changed but her waistline.
She was proud, truth be told. And why not? She had lost
sixty-five pounds over the course of a year, so that between
the ages of sixteen and seventeen she'd gone from being
a pudgy, 260-pound duck of a girl to someone who could
almost pass for a video dancer. A background dancer,

maybe—all booty shot and no close-up—but still. She prided herself on her unconventional thinking, whatever that was worth, and she had never claimed "video ho" as one of her life's ambitions. Still, it was nice to mark the accomplishment. It was the kind of thing a mother would take note of, Shaniece imagined—"look at my daughter, slimming down so nice," a certain kind of mother might say—though Shaniece really couldn't know.

When Harlem's street men started to holler at her, it felt glorious, mostly. She felt their eyes wrapping around her hips as she walked, coaxing her new body left and right like music. She let herself talk to some of them—the young ones, and the ones with decent smiles. Sometimes she gave out her number. Once in a while she talked to the boys and let them do her clumsily on top of the thinning pink comforter on her twin bed. She felt like she had been beamed up and welcomed into a world of skinny-girl splendor, enfolded in a universe of actual womanhood she never thought she'd see in her little fat-girl life. As thrilling as the men's eyes sometimes felt on her, it was this—feeling like a woman, finally—that was the true gift.

That was the feeling that overcame her when her best friend's father came over to return the camera he'd borrowed from her father. Her father was at work at the Home and Office Depot, and her mother was wherever she'd disappeared to when Shaniece was five—some home in some place called Sosúa in the Dominican Republic, according to the birthday cards that arrived every other year or so, signed "Patricia Guzmán" in a distracted scrawl, sometimes a month after her birthday. No one talked about Patricia Guzmán except her father, who occasionally came home after a night of drinking and groaned about how beautiful she was, his eyes glassy with gin. Shaniece never answered the cards. Instead, she soothed herself with fantasies of who Patricia might be, what kind of men loved her, and how. She tried not to wonder why she'd vanished without leaving so much as a glamorous photo behind. This was what a woman would do, Shaniece resolved: accept the facts and move on. On the day of her best friend's father's visit, there was no one in the apartment to bother her or tell her "no," no one to say "he's grown" or "girl, you not a woman yet," which she wouldn't have wanted to hear anyway. He wore a suit and tie. He had a nice smile. He smelled like cigarette smoke, but also chewing gum and cologne. He had always been nice to her, and that night, he gave her the woman feeling in waves.

There was no no, *and no need to say it. Feeling like a woman meant doing what you wanted, whyever you wanted to do it. It meant not worrying about why and being glad for the chance to do it, glad for the chance, glad past words, so much glad the* yes *was your body. There was no* no *and there was no* yes, *and what there was was feeling, but if you asked her what the feelings were, she probably couldn't tell you, which didn't matter anyway 'cause it's not like anyone asked.*

The first few days after his visit, Shaniece felt all kinds of different. There were the expected changes: she found herself walking straighter and taller, strutting with less effort, noticing the roundness of her own hips mid-swish. She felt more confident. Not in the tired Ricki Lake talk show sense of the word, women snapping their fingers in geometric patterns and rolling their necks into knots. No. She felt confident in a more literal sense: she found herself asking fewer questions, spending less time prevaricating on details like what to wear to work at the C-Town supermarket on Broadway, or whether she could get away with filing her nails under her register. She had bagged a man like this, after all—the furthest thing from a street dude, a grown man with a good job and nice teeth. She must have been doing something right. She wondered what Patricia Guzmán might say.

But soon other changes followed—stranger, quieter ones that crept up slowly after he left that night and began to hover over her days. She found herself distracted, forgetful in ways totally unlike her. She had never had the luxury of absentmindedness—she took pride in holding things down while her father was at work, contributing to rent with her wages from C-Town, making sure there were tasty and nutritious dinners made, cleaning the apartment as best she could, and all the while keeping up with her homework. After the visit, the fastidious, *get-things-done* part of her went dormant, and she found it hard to focus on even simple things. After he left that night, she tried to clean up as she usually did when she had boys over, clearing the apartment of evidence and leaving her father's mess just so. But this time she forgot one thing. When her father came home and found two Newport Light butts in the empty tuna can that passed for an ashtray, he held it in her face and said, "Who you have over here? Only person I know smokes these candy sticks is your mother."

The forgetfulness got worse after that. First she forgot small, unimportant things—whether she'd pressed the button for her floor on the elevator or how soon she'd have to turn the stove off before her cauliflower burned. But soon it became a problem. Some days she sat at her register for full minutes trying to remember her employee code. Once she complained to Mr. Orlando, the elderly tenement super, that her keys had stopped working, only to realize she'd been trying to use the bottom key in the top lock. After letting her into the apartment, Mr. Orlando shook his head and gave her a soft, wet-eyed look she'd only seen him give the building's crack addicts. "You take care of yourself, Shawnie," he said. "With no woman in the house, your father needs you."

She could not describe this combination of quickness and distraction, even if there had been someone to describe it to, which there wasn't. She had learned to consider strength and resilience as among her defining features, for better or worse. But this new feeling pressed on her, and even a week after the visit she couldn't will it away. She felt like a heavy thing sent hurling across the air, liable to change direction at any moment. Unsteady and unstoppable. Unwieldy. She went to school and to work and kept up with her assignments, but between tasks she moved like a rush of steam, her body thinned to vapors, without much to say to anyone, and nothing to say to her friend. She had to heave forward as quickly as possible, through each moment, each conversation, each day, or she would be swallowed up into space.

By the second week after the visit, she had to scrunch her face and narrow her eyes each time she went to the bathroom to keep from seeing the strange look of herself in the mirror. At work, she stood bolt-stiff at the register with her back to the glass store window, picking methodically at her flaking nail polish between transactions to remind herself she was still there. She did everything she could to avoid seeing her reflection, but if you asked her why she'd have to say *I don't know*.

It was this unsteadiness, this never knowing, that Shaniece wasn't able to shake. It messed with her, messed her up. Partly because it wasn't like her and partly because she didn't know what it would make her do. Sometimes she found herself standing at her register, staring at the sticky rolling belt, wishing she could shrink herself down and ride it down, down, away.

There was no one she could talk to about this. The girls at school had mostly written her off as either a pig or a weirdo, and she didn't need the girls from her building up in her business. There were a few girls at the C-Town who might understand, but they were suspicious of her because she'd slept with Javarious, the twenty-something junior manager, and what do a ho's weird feelings matter, anyway? She couldn't talk to her best friend because she wasn't her best friend anymore.

During this time, Shaniece didn't think of her friend's father's visit, of the smells or the sounds or the things she had said and the things she hadn't. Sometimes she thought of the feelings, but they confused her and made her want to disappear. She thought mostly of one person: Patricia Guzmán. Patricia Guzmán of the lightning-bolt vanishing, of the trampled envelopes and the half-life's worth of birthday love. Patricia Guzmán, whose defining feature was that she was gone.

Shaniece had resolved, way back in the bodega-lunch days of elementary school, that it was okay for a black girl not to have a father. It was the logic that governed Harlem and, she was sure, much of the world. It was a fact that shaped everything from talk show plots to public policy, and even gave her her last name: she was only a Guzmán because at the time of her birth there was no reason to think the young Jerome Armistice would stick around. It had always seemed to Shaniece that the logic of black-girl fatherlessness, if tragic, had its silver lining. A fatherless black girl meant a black girl with a mother worth her weight in gold, a mother larger than dreams, who boldly rode the lip of martyrdom and escaped devastation at every pass. Most importantly, a fatherless black girl had a mother who was present, ever, always, overwhelmingly present, administering rigorous and inescapable instruction in all that a woman is and must be. Absent fathers could be forgotten with a sour suck of the teeth, proof of society's decay, the downfall of the race, whatever. But if a black girl didn't have a mother, questions would arise. What kind of woman leaves her daughter? Why? What kind of woman will the girl turn out to be?

Shaniece had made her life around avoiding these questions, making herself quiet to the point of invisibility and sharing her secrets with almost no one. But now she had questions of her own. For all the wondering she'd done about Patricia Guzmán, she had never wondered deep enough, not deep enough to imagine what speeding weight, what unbearable, dizzy distraction, would make a woman want to disappear.

Now, she didn't need to imagine. She needed to tell, to ask.

She pulled a rickety chair to the kitchen table, ripped a sheet off her father's dusty legal pad, and wrote, hoping and not hoping her mother would understand.

WHAT DOES
FORGIVENESS MEAN?

BY JOLIE HOLLAND

WHEN I WAS A CHILD, boys and men often mocked me for speaking. I developed a fear of speaking that haunts me to this day.

When I was seven, a teenage relative showed me his dick twitching in his jeans. The same relative, who was also physically violent and unremittingly inappropriate with kids my age, also sexually assaulted one of our young female relatives. One female legal guardian kept the assault secret from the boy's father because she knew his father would beat him if he found out. She chose to protect the abuser rather than the abused. I heard about the assault as an adult.

When I was nine, my stepparent's brother tried to take off my pants. I didn't tell anyone because there was no one I could trust.

At the age of twelve, a substitute teacher asked if I had a boyfriend and acted surprised when I said I didn't. He told me I was just the kind of girl he would have liked to date if he were my age. I didn't tell anyone about what he said because there was no one I could trust.

When I was thirteen and having what I now recognize as significant symptoms of physiological stress, my mother took me to see a doctor. In his office, in front of my mother, he made snide sexual comments to me. My mother said nothing about it to him or to me. I barely understood his statements until years later.

About the same time, a teenage neighbor boy sent my legal guardian a letter telling her he was jerking off at my bedroom window. She never told me if she did anything about it, such as communicate with his parents or the authorities. As far as I know, she didn't.

On another occasion, a strange man cornered me while I was walking through my neighborhood in the evening and held a gun to my head. I was with a pack of kids my age. The man didn't discharge his gun. We all managed to run away. None of us told any adults what had happened.

At the age of thirteen, I was sexually assaulted by a stranger, an adult man. I didn't tell anyone because there was no one I could trust. I came home and cleaned up, looked myself in the eye, and told myself I was alright.

All of these things happened before I was fourteen, and I never told any adults. I lived in a "safe" part of town.

It's hard, now, to imagine how I maintained my silence. I have good, close friends and I like to verbally process any crazy thing that happens to me. That I repressed my feelings at thirteen after being sexually assaulted, or after a grown man held a pistol to my temple, is unthinkable to me now. But then I remember how I was mocked when I spoke in those days. I remember my fear of speaking and my actions make more sense.

*   *   *

When I was seventeen, my boyfriend picked up a heavy piece of furniture and whacked me over the head with it. He and I had been planning on going to college together across the country. I had grants and scholarships to a prestigious university, but I dropped them out of fear. I didn't want to be forced to see him regularly.

In my late teens, I visited some friends in a nearby town and spent the night in a motel. Some men banged on my door. I heard them muttering about raping me. I called the police because I was scared. A lady cop showed up and questioned me, but not the men. She yelled at me for wasting her time.

In my early twenties, I got into a little fight with my boyfriend. He took off in a huff around midnight, and I left shortly afterwards to try to find him. This was before cell phones. The streets were deserted. I saw only one other person on the street, a clean-cut, expensively dressed young white man. He approached me and asked about the transit system. I answered his questions, then continued walking away from my boyfriend's house. Eventually I decided to turn around and go wait for my boyfriend to come home. It slowly dawned on me that the stranger had changed course and was following me. He was three or four blocks behind me when he began yelling, describing how he was going to kill me. I screamed back and cursed at him so he would know I'd put up a fight if he got too close. Terrified to lead the man back to my boyfriend's empty house, I got to a better-lit part of the street and found a homeless guy. I stopped to talk with him for a minute so that I'd at least have a witness if the screaming man caught up to me. I asked the homeless man to walk me a couple blocks to my boyfriend's house so it would appear I was not alone. He refused.

In the moment that I'd stopped to talk to the homeless man, the guy who was chasing me disappeared from view. I could no longer see his silhouette in the distance on the darkened streets. I took the chance to run toward my boyfriend's house, hoping the man could not see me from some hidden vantage point in the darkness.

I managed to get back to my boyfriend's house safely, checked that all the doors were locked, and turned off every light so no one could see inside. I got a sharp knife from the kitchen and crouched in the dark, straining my ears after every creak in the old house, every little sound in the neighborhood. My boyfriend came home drunk about an hour later.

I didn't call the cops because my boyfriend was growing a pot plant in his closet.

A friend of mine was nearly murdered by a rock star. She didn't press charges at the time because she was a young drug addict and he was a hugely famous man.

My ex-girlfriend was raped by dozens of men on one occasion. She didn't go to the cops because she was a sex worker.

Friends of friends were raped by cops. They didn't press charges because they knew how it would go in court.

None of those men ever came to justice.

I have a friend who barely escaped a mass murderer. She didn't go to the cops at the time because she was a homeless teenager, but the man was later caught and convicted for murdering other women. He'll die in prison now.

A male ex-friend sexually assaulted one of my female friends. Another male ex-friend sexually coerced one of my female friends. Another male ex-friend shoved one of my female friends down some stairs. An ex-friend's bandmate brutally raped one of my female friends. My ex-friend refused to support our friend who had been raped because he would have had to call the cops to come to his house.

Two of those women "forgave" the men who hurt them. I put the word in quotation marks because I literally don't know what forgiveness means in those cases.

Does it mean "I know you're trash and I expected that of you"?

Does it mean "I perceive myself as trash and I don't care how you treat me"?

When I walk alone in any city, in any neighborhood, I am sexually harassed. If I step ten feet away from my band while on tour, I am sexually harassed. It has been this way since I was ten. Not two hours ago, while I was walking alone in Los Angeles, a man stared me down. I held my head up high, like Lou Reed says, and didn't make eye contact. As I passed the man, he turned and stared pointedly at me.

This behavior is recognized as aggression in social animals. You don't stare an unknown dog in the face. That's fighting words.

I was on tour when I was writing this, editing these paragraphs on my phone while waiting in an airport. I looked up to find another strange man staring at me, sustaining eye contact for no damn good reason.

SIX POEMS

BY LYNN MELNICK

—

LANDSCAPE WITH GREYHOUND AND GREASEWOOD

MOSTLY MEN KEEP SINGING
while dark blood collects where I open

and I line my polka dot panties with rest stop receipts.

I think probably we'll pause in Barstow to continue
these lyrics

but I'm no standard:

I fold over to smell myself.

Route 66 to Las Vegas.
Perfect for a child and also America

loves the promise of a long haul.

I pull the tab from a small can of apple juice:
see?

I'm cared for.
The man next to me puts his hand on my thigh.

He gets the kind of girl I am,
new leaves shiny with oil, flammable.

Come on.

Know better. Somebody,
know better.

LANDSCAPE WITH SMUT AND PAVEMENT

AT NIGHT I HALLUCINATE THE grunting discord

which leapt from a human body as he destroyed mine.
That very month, I obliterated a beetle on a shiny walkway.

That month was November.

I think they are all out to get me,
all the insects in their armor.

Some folks like to use the word *slut,* even with children.

I am holding all my blood in vials on my lap.

The splatter is delicate.
I guess I am bleeding all over the scenery.

I was born in November.

But you want to hear about the clean stretch of pavement
where a beetle once lived

or the surrounding archways that were the kind of architecture
that bodies who have been treated gently like to enjoy.

The kempt lawn was always kempt.
I was disparaged on that terrain.

I was smut.
The rest was burnished.

HISTORICAL ACCURACY

SAY IT'S THE '80s
and we're all wearing a whole lot of electric pink.

And I'm wearing it short.

I'm wearing it swimsuit, nowhere near the water.

I hire a skywriter to describe me:
voluptuous, terrified, bewitching, willing to wait

Somewhere in my schoolbooks it says to avoid
big crowds and flying objects

it says to check my work carefully
before the creep

with the grease-stained cuticles and menthol breath
does what he believes he was put in front of me to do

because
the skywriter got confused and wrote:

terrified, showstopping, mute, asking for it

No one in this town is surprised by the error,
they frown as I am always

pulling some sort of airshow
from the comfort of my crappy apartment.

But when the creep hits the field
to duck and cover

and the others scatter
with their hands over their visors over their eyes

and the plane crashes
headlong into the middle

of a more serious set of adjectives,
I'm pretty sure that the best solution here

is to get out of the '80s

and join the young Republicans pulling together
amid all the rubble.

LANDSCAPE
WITH LOANWORD
AND SOLSTICE

SAY YES

so I let him run me to the limits

in a pickup though I know better
than to expect

the chaparral
to grow much through trauma

except in order to withstand
extinction

though it appears
under the smog

supernatural.

CUT TO: he shoves my face
into the flatbed then punts me

when he's filled me.
Walk home and I do,

scrub for miles
the darkest day of the year moving in

and out of comprehension
but I am glad

(hear me? I am glad)
because now it can be over.

LANDSCAPE WITH WRITTEN STATEMENT

YOU WRAP MY RIBS in gauze—
an experiment with the word *tenderly*

after your hands left my throat too bruised to speak.

While winter sun squints at the ghost flower
dying in its shabby terra cotta

far from home

men tell me to be honest about my role in the incident:

Okay, yes
I should have stayed inside

while you railed from the sidewalk

but my confused heart got into the car.

What happened is
I once spent too much time in the desert

so pogonip seems glamorous hung stuck in the trees
like when blood dries on skin

and I want to wear it

out for an evening,
pat my hands over its kinky path down my face

because: fuck you,

you didn't find me here.
I brought you here.

SOME IDEAS FOR
EXISTING IN PUBLIC

I THINK YOU SHOULD GRIP your dick through your jeans
    and ask me

if I can handle it because you know I can, right?
I'm here for you.

I think you should overtake me at a bus bench

and invite me to sit on your face.
I think you should track me down

the block and clarify how you'd like to split my slit open

until I pass out.

(Once, as a kid, I was balancing on a ledge
all morning thinking no one

could see me until a man walked by and captured my chin
    in his grip
and called me *dollface*.)

I think you should screw me sideways right here on the
    sidewalk
like you said you might like to screw me

sideways before you took off
past the cop who said it's pointless to prove the crime so

come on, sure, screw me sideways, and why just sideways
why not all ways? Why not diagonal?

I think you should whistle so loud at my fat ass
that I jump like a stray rodent and you couldn't be more
     correct

it is a shame my fat ass is walking away

from you because why is it walking away from you?
Why am I walking away from you? Why am I here on the
     sidewalk?

I'm yours.

LAKES

BY CAITLIN DELOHERY

STILL, YEARS LATER, AFTER sleepless nights filled with flashbacks, after leaving the city I loved like family to get away from this story or because I couldn't tell this story, after my life split in two because of this story, split and started over again, still, I question whether there's anything to tell, and if there is, whether I have the right to tell it.

In 2006, my cousin Danny shot his girlfriend 16 times. Her name was Sarah and she was 25 years old, the same age I was at the time.

Daniel Patrick Walsh, 33, shot and killed his girlfriend 16 times with a Glock. He had just gotten back from Iraq.

My cousin, the boy who put a certain darkness in me, grew up to be the man who beat every woman he loved.

I've been writing my cousin's story for the past decade. I've written it over and over and over again. Even that sentence—*I've been writing my cousin's story for the past decade*—isn't quite true. It's *my* story, it's the story of the woman he murdered, it's the story of another angry white man in America with a gun, it's the story of another angry teenage boy alone with a little girl and his cock.

My cousin is in prison because he shot his girlfriend 16 times. She was sitting on the toilet when it happened, the newspaper said, an ungenerous detail to report, one I have never gotten out of my mind—both the fact of it and the reporting of it.

It's not lovely. I've always struggled with that—this is not a pretty story. And what I mean by that is that I'm sorry for telling you this story. I want to both protect you from it and in some way force you to see it, in all its ugliness.

In 2006, my cousin shot his girlfriend 16 times. He shot her in the heart, in the head, and in her vagina. They had just had sex. After, he called his mother, who called a priest before she called the police. She said that my cousin tried to kill himself after he'd done it, but the gun jammed.

The woman he killed was named Sarah. She was a nursing student, and she was only 25 years old.

For the past decade—that's not quite right either. There were barren years, too, when I wasn't writing—this story or any other. Four years without any words at all. The first year, I constantly had an image of myself submerged in a blue lake, under thick, clear ice. My sitting-in-my-apartment self could look down and see this drowning self, pressing her hands and face against the ice, again and again.

I can't draw you a diagram of what my cousin did to me a couple decades before he killed a woman. I can't name all of what I saw or was made to touch or do or accept. I can't tell you how many years it went on, list the number of times. I can't tell you how my kid body responded, recoiled, or how it didn't. Often, the clearest way I can understand myself, now, at thirty-seven, at twenty-seven when I first started writing this story, and at four years old, when I think this story began for me, is to remind myself, aloud or in writing, just: something happened.

Something happened that divided my life into a before and after, or, because there was so little before, made my early life something other than just a child's life. Something happened before I had a language for it, something happened that I couldn't name for a long time and still struggle to name. Something happened that is defined by certain images and sensations, certain visceral leaps and dead zones, that come up again and again:

I see my cousin's face as a teenager, a smile and a frown both flickering on his face, like those hologram cards we used to have as kids.

I see his eyes, I see his mouth, I remember or imagine the pee smell of him, the pee smell of him on me, hot and wet and choking, fleece pajamas pressed against my stomach, pee-soaked fleece pajamas a gag around my girl-mouth.

I see his unmade bed, I remember or imagine a certain fleshy, squeaky sound and a medical rubber color on the corner of a mattress.

I feel the brown vertigo of my grandparents' waterbed, the cold blue slosh of water, the panic of not being able to get up from it, moored in the very center.

I see his mother's—my aunt's—dirty kitchen. I smell a can of creamed corn, the sweet-rotten-deathy gag of creamed corn.

I see dim light on dark, too-shiny wood, like the exoskeleton of those fat Manhattan cockroaches that tormented me when I first lived in the city.

And, always, I see the writhing of pink faceless creatures, their bodies segmented and endless, and feel a stuck, unmoving panic at the sinister intelligence of their squirming.

Lake Stillwell is a man-made lake, brown in the summer and gray in wintertime, edged by condos, two of which my grandparents owned. When my cousins and I were kids, our parents would stand out on the astroturfed decks and drink and smoke and laugh and argue. My cousins and I fished off of the tiny dock just beneath them and dug crawdads out of the mud on the shore with our fingers. I loved to catch fish but was terrified of their out-of-control, death-throes bodies once I got them on the line. Danny used to take my fish off the hook for me. We would lay them on the dock and watch them die in the sun. I remember the bright mirrored precision of their silver scales, the round wet O of their mouths, the shocking pink when they fanned their gills out, gasping for air.

When I write the story of my cousin, I always try to trace the lines from what he did to me to the crime that landed him in prison for almost the rest of his life: *my cousin hurt me—my cousin killed a girl just my age, my cousin hurt me—my cousin beat every woman he loved, my cousin hurt me—my cousin shot a woman he said he loved, shot her so many times, like he wished he could kill her more than once*. Though they are his crimes, for a long time they felt like mine. I would draw that line again and again from what he did to me to what he did to Sarah and think: if only I had told someone sooner, if only I had made a bigger deal of it, if only I had insisted something was wrong, then maybe he could've been stopped, maybe all of this could have been prevented. Because I knew all along that there was something dark as death in him. I knew because he put his darkness in me.

*   *   *

Last summer, we spent most weekends at a sprawling man-made lake just north of Portland, the city I moved back to after I tried to leave this story in Brooklyn. The lake is called Blue Lake but the water is green, green like the sea in a storybook. There's a little roped-off area for kids to swim in. Gold flecks of mica swirl around us, giving the sun to us in miniature, by the dozen, by the handful. Everything is technicolor, our eyes still shocked by full color after nine months of gray and muted green. One weekend, Quinn—my girlfriend's niece, our foster daughter, who came to us when she was four years old—surveys her lake kingdom from the throne of her inner tube. Again and again, she dives into the water for me to catch her when she comes up for air, and I'm entranced by the moment just before she surfaces, the dome of water framing her singular face, the little bubbles of her breath and the mica both floating across her wild smile, her feral eyes closed as if in prayer.

A few times, I slip away, on the other side of the rope, where it's too deep to reach the bottom, and faceless, swaying things brush against the soles of my feet. I try to hold my panic in check when Quinn is watching. I think that's what I'm doing—floating on my back with the sun on my face, a rare golden calm layered on top of a crawling fear of what might be underneath—when a young man slips into the lake a few hundred feet away and drowns.

I could tell you about what happens next—how we stood dripping in our bathing suits while a reporter tried to interview us about water safety, how the light of our little summer day seemed to bruise with emergency. How I couldn't shake the feeling that I'd swallowed some small particles of death, of his last breath. How his death felt like a reminder of something I still can't name.

But let's stay here in the shallow end, where the sun hits the water just right, with Quinn shapeshifting in quick turns—she's a mermaid, she's the president, she's a doctor-chef-hairdresser—shivering, laughing in my arms. Let's stay here where she is unaware of the boy being dragged from the lake bottom, and where I don't know how he'll haunt me, how I won't be able to get out of my mind the image of the green water closed all around me, flecked with gold, the light at the surface near but unreachable.

NIGHTINGALE:
A GLOSS

BY PAISLEY REKDAL

Nay, then I'll stop your mouth.

—Shakespeare, *Titus Andronicus, II, iii*

LANGUAGE IS THE FIRST site of loss and our first defense against it. Which is why after Philomela's brother-in-law, Tereus, rapes her, he cuts out her tongue and tosses it, the bloody stump writhing at her feet.

*   *   *

In my poem "Philomela," I leave out this mutilation. Strike out Philomela's sister, Procne, who learns of her sister's rape from the tapestry Philomela weaves. Cut the death of Itys, Procne's son, whom the sisters dismember and boil for punishment, Philomela, mute but grinning, tossing the boy's head at his father. No metamorphosis of Philomela and Procne into nightingale and swallow, Tereus shrunk into the hoopoe that pursues them. Such details would be unimaginable, I think. Not because a contemporary reader can't imagine them, but because the details are now too grotesque for her to want to.

*   *   *

Ovid makes the trio's transformation occur at the instant syntax shifts from the conditional to the imperfect. "[The girls] went flying.../ [as] if they were on wings. They were on wings!" he writes. The difference between simile and metaphor. The second the mouth conceives it, the imagination turns it into the real.

        —The Metamorphoses, 6.669–670

*   *   *

I'm writing "Philomela" at an artists' colony where I go for daily runs. Sometimes a man in a car will pace me; sometimes a man on his bike will circle back to get another look. Sometimes the men who pass me say nothing.

Around this residency are woods in which, the staff informs us, we can walk. It is beautiful here, and there are olive groves. I do not walk by myself in the woods.

*   *   *

It's 1992 and I'm hiking near Loch Ness. It's just after breakfast: I've spent the morning alone in a stand of gold aspen that circles the lake. When the three men find me, the smell of beer and whiskey thick on their clothes, bait boxes and fishing rods in hand, I have just sat down with a book. The men are red-eyed, gruff. The first two nod as they pass me: it is the third who walks back. He has lank, gingery hair, and black spots in his teeth.

Hello, he says when he reaches me.

*   *   *

Nightingale: OE *nihtegala, niht + galan*, small, reddish-brown migratory bird celebrated for its sweet night song during the breeding season. In Dutch, a frog.

* * *

Virgil, *The Georgics*, Book IV:
> [A]s mourning beneath the poplar shade the
>   nightingale
> laments her lost brood... she sobs
> nightlong, and on a branch perched her doleful song
> renews—"

* * *

Shelley, *A Defence of Poetry*: "A poet is a nightingale who sits in darkness, and sings to cheer its solitude with sweet sounds; his auditors are as men entranced by the melody of an unseen musician."

* * *

Are you an American? he asks. I always wanted to kiss an American.

*   *   *

Female nightingales do not sing. Only the male sings, as Tereus does, attempting to woo Philomela with words. "Love made him eloquent," Ovid writes, suggesting that Tereus' language is aroused by Philomela's silence. What space is a woman? "[S]ome Pallas in place which furthered my inuention, for I am in that point of Ouid his opinion, that, *Si cupia sponte disertus erit* (desire makes a man spontaneously eloquent)." A palace of pleasure arousing both erotic and narrative desires.

> —George Pettie, *A Petite Pallace of Pettie his Pleasure*, 1576.

*   *   *

Just a kiss, he says, dropping his tackle box, and I know I should run. He grabs my head, and I am already clawing at his neck, terrified for myself but also terrified of hurting him. Hurting him will make it worse for me. He hisses in my ear as I slap his hands, and now he's got his arms around me. I rear back, unbalancing myself, so that when I do the one thing I've been taught, which is to bring my right knee up hard into his groin, the blow is too weak.

That didn't work, I stammer, as my leg grazes the inside of his thigh.

It never does, he replies. And now he has me on the ground.

*   *   *

Philomel, Philomela: ME, from Greek *Philo+melos*, song, a nightingale.

Matthew Arnold, "Philomela": How thick the bursts come crowding through the leaves!

> Again—thou hearest!
> Eternal passion!
> Eternal pain!

*   *   *

I do not use my voice. Two other men are ahead of us in the woods: I have no idea what they will do if called back, where their allegiances will lie. As if these were rules agreed upon, he doesn't shout either. In retrospect, his silence suggests that his friends might have taken my side. But at that moment, the two of us cajole and beg and threaten in hisses. The whole attack is conducted in silence.

*   *   *

Ovid says it is imagination that makes possible this sudden turn towards violence: Tereus "sees beyond what he sees," an idea embroidered on by later writers. "[H]ee seemed to see her stand apparently before him (only a strong imagination assurynge him that it was shee) which sight sunk so deeply into his heart and brought him such excessiue delight, that hee presently awakened, and missing the partie that procured him such pleasure, his ioy was turned to anoy," writes George Pettie in his rewriting of the myth. To see past what we know into what we desire, to put that desire into language. And by performing that, to enact in the reader a similar performance. The art is not complete until we imagine the outcome for ourselves.

—A Petite Pallace of Pettie his Pleasure.
—The Metamorphoses, 6.453–482

*   *   *

My hands are pushed up against his chest, his hands are in my pants, on my breasts. He says nothing, though he grimaces, his face close to my own as he leans to kiss me so that I whip my head away. I can feel the cold leaves against my cheek, the damp earth, can spy my book lying a few feet off. *Just let him,* something small, dry, miserable in me says. *Let him, and it will all be over.* But I don't. I keep my mouth shut, and I fight.

*   *   *

There is no scream after the tongue is cut, but would we hear a cry? Philomela screams only in the text, thus in our minds: in that, her body and our own do not communicate. We *cannot* hear her. We want to, but she exists only in our imagination: an absent body that exists in the past or an unforeseeable future. She begs for help we can never give.

It is absurd to suggest we could. In that sense, she never needed a tongue to scream for help. She never had one.

—K. Frances Lieder, "*Lights Out* and an Ethics of Spectatorship: Or, Can the Subaltern Scream?"

*　　*　　*

The rape isn't described in my poem "Philomela": it takes place off stage, recorded years after the event by the character who experienced it. I left out the rape, thinking to reject a reader's voyeurism. But the reader of myths knows what is left out: my silence, then, is not a revision but an invitation to imagine, to remember, this violence for yourself.

*　　*　　*

Procne, too, must imagine her sister's violation. Philomela's weaving thus becomes a muslin veil drawn over experience, both bringing her sister in, and shutting her out.

*　　*　　*

And then his fingers are tearing inside me, his tongue filling my own mouth.

*   *   *

The woods are ruthless, dreadful, deaf, and dull;
There speak, and strike, brave boys, and take your turns;
There serve your lusts, shadow'd from heaven's eye,
And revel in Lavinia's treasury.
　　　—*Titus Andronicus,* II, i

*   *   *

He stops. He withdraws his hand from my pants, lets go my hair. I curl my legs up into my chest as he pushes himself, unsteadily, off me. That wasn't much, was it? he asks. He brushes leaves off his clothes.

*   *   *

When I try and explain what his teeth looked like, what his breath smelled like, the cold ridges of his nails as they clawed inside me, I know I am asking for something beyond the response of your own suffering, your awareness of my suffering. I don't care what you know or how you feel. I want to go back in time, to an eternal *before*. I want you to give me what no one can give me. Which is why, for many years, I have resisted talking about it.

*   *   *

Tongue: OE *tunge* + Latin *lingua*: an organ of speech, a figure or representation of this organ; the faculty of speech. A voice, a vote, suffrage.

To assail with words; to cut a tongue; to slit or shape a tongue in a plant for grafting.

"Giving Great Tongue": a cry made by hounds when they scent a fox.

*   *   *

"Will not my tongue be mute?" Tarquin wonders, at the thought of raping Lucretia. The momentary horror he experiences believing that the rape must mark him as well: a blot upon his face as well as language, violence carving its sin upon his own self. If she cannot go unmarked, he cannot either; the body giving tongue to its distress.

—Shakespeare, "The Rape of Lucrece," 227

*   *   *

It is not rape, and yet. Sexual violence has been historically difficult to articulate. Chaucer devoted much of the fifth book of "The Legend of Good Women," in which he retells the myth of Philomela, to creating subcategories of words akin to rape: *ravine,* a rape linked with abduction; *robberie,* a rape occurring in the woods; *stelthe,* an attack cloaked in secrecy. We would not care to make such distinctions, but Chaucer's characters do. When Amans (Latin: "Loving") is asked whether or not he has committed the sin of ravine, he denies it, admitting only to the possibility of stelthe. It is important, he demands, to be specific. What happened to me feels like something that exists between words, a subcategory of expression for which there is no one easy expression.

Ravine: OF *raviner* + L. *rapinare:* to pillage, sweep down, to violently sweep away.

*   *   *

Raving: MF *resver,* to wander, to be delirious. "Raving" is applied to the Bacchantes or Maenads, whose name means "raving ones." Procne first appears in Ovid's tale dressed as the Bacchantes' queen, "in all the dress/ of frenzy," spear over her shoulder, draped in vines and deer hide. Philomela, voiceless suffering, is visited by her sister, rage. A raping. A raving.
   —*The Metamorphoses*, 6.589-590

*   *   *

"Raving:" at the heart of the story is madness, a word sonically, if not etymologically, attached to the word for rape. Raving is a contagion that spreads through imagination and desire. To the ancient writers, only raving breeds and explains female aggression. Agave, driven mad by Dionysus for her "unbridled tongue," doesn't know her son, Pentheus, spikes his head on a stake. Medea, to punish an unfaithful Jason, dismembers their children. To wound one is to wound the other, bodies linked by sperm and milk and blood. Don't infect me with your madness.
   —Euripides, *The Bacchae*, l. 438

*　　*　　*

If art is the eloquence left Philomela, what answer does it inspire? Pain speaks to pain. "Why should one make pretty speeches and the other be dumb?" Procne wonders, looking back and forth between Philomela's tapestry and her son. Itys' ability to speak throws Philomela's silence into loud relief, and though he says nothing in the myth, his flesh "keeps something of the spirit alive." When Procne dismembers him, he "leaps in the boiling water, hisses on the turning skewers." Pain, too, is a language. It raves in me with a diabolic tongue.

　　　—*The Metamorphoses*, 6.647-649
　　　—Czeslaw Milosz, "Language"

*　　*　　*

Rape is the dark seam of *The Metamorphoses*. To Ovid, a poet, perhaps the ultimate dehumanizing act would bring the body to a place beyond language. People in his versions of the myths often become animals, men and women "more cut off from words than a seal," as Robert Lowell wrote of one manic stint spent in McLean. To live cut off from words is to descend into the bodily, the irrational. It is, if words make law and government, to be outside of political power. To make his (literate, male) audience understand such powerlessness, Ovid frames the rape from Philomela's point of view. He centers male agency within a silent female consciousness.

—Robert Lowell, "Waking in the Blue," 24

* * *

But if you stubbornly keep lying down in bed, dressed,
    You'll feel my hands by way of your torn dress:
In fact, if my anger should carry me further,
    You'll show wounded arms to your mother.
—Propertius 2.15.17–20

* * *

Or Ovid features rape because it is a trope of Roman elegiac discourse. *Arma, amor, ira.* Either way, desire is scripted by violence.

* * *

Madness to insist upon narrative cohesion when the story is one of fragmentation, chaos. The story is one of raving. Philomela's descent is an unveiling of the animal heart at the world's center. The girl, running as if flying into the woods. The girl flying. Tereus crystallized in the body of a spike-crowned predator. If we become the thing which symbolizes us, it is not change then, but revelation.

*   *   *

[Tereus] was a passionate man, and all the Thracians
    are quick at loving...
    Two fires burned in him: his own passion and his nation's.

*   *   *

To Ovid, violence is brute, natural, indifferent; it wells up in men's blood, a moral emptiness that obeys no rules because it understands none. In *The Metamorphoses*, the truth of violence is that it might erupt at any time: the void always threatens to yawn before us, and we struggle to assemble words that will explain it. Only language, which orders time and gives experience shape and meaning, might control how violence is experienced. It gives back agency. "There was no time ever/ when she would rather have had the use of her tongue,/ the power to speak, to express her full rejoicing," Ovid writes, after Philomela throws Itys' bloody head at Tereus' feet. Language is made to contain our awareness of, even our celebration in, suffering. The pain attending our pleasure. The pleasure we take in another's pain.

— *The Metamorphoses*, 6.460–462, 659–661

*   *   *

Here are the words describing Philomela's cut tongue: *immurmurat* (murmurs), *palpitat* (quivers), *quaerit* (strives). Like a lover, the tongue murmurs, it quivers, it strives for its mistress.

— *The Metamorphoses*, 6.562–564

*   *   *

Positioning an implicitly male audience in the consciousness of a raving, raped woman tilts the myth from one of identification to one of rejection. To portray Philomela's calls for justice within the frame of madness reduces her moral justification for Tereus' punishment. It focuses the reader's gaze back upon her mutilated body, her tortured mind, turning our regard from one of empathy to spectacle.

*   *   *

Keats, in his copy of *Titus Andronicus*, a play that rewrites the myth of Philomela, struck out with his pen several of the taunting lines spoken by Demetrius and Chiron after they've raped Lavinia, sliced out her tongue and cut off her hands. He drew his pen vigorously over their dialogue, mutilating their speech: violence overwriting violence.

*   *   *

MARCUS

Speak, gentle niece, what stern ungentle hands
Have lopp'd and hew'd and made thy body bare
Of her two branches, those sweet ornaments—

*   *   *

In Julie Taymore's *Titus*, Lavinia wears branches for hands, recalling Shakespeare's recurring metaphor: Lavinia's hands "tremble, like aspen-leaves, upon a lute"; Chiron, sneering, suggests her "stumps will let [her] play the scribe." Wood as scene of violation, wood as body, body as failed writing instrument. Lavinia's changes, too, are metonymic. *The girls run as if they are flying. They are flying!*

　　—*Titus Andronicus,* II, iv

*   *   *

Branch: ME also F *branche*, a tree limb or stem, a child, also (fig) a division; to strike out on a new path; to divide.

　　Hew: OE *haewan*, to strike forcefully, to cut, to shape, to slaughter.

　　Limb: OT *limo-*, organ or part of the body; limb (L, *limbus*), an edge or boundary of a surface.

*   *   *

Near an olive grove by the residency lives a bird which mimics human song. An opera singer stands there certain afternoons, dust in the tall grasses, heat bringing out the scent of lemon and jasmine. She sings into the field where the unseen bird nests, a tree branch swaying under its small body. The bird waits a beat after she finishes, then— matching her note for note—trills back. Try it yourself, she says, charmed by the idea of speaking across species. Perhaps a mating call. Perhaps a delineation of territory.

*   *   *

Keats returned often to the figure of the nightingale: a symbol common to the Romantic poets.

"Ode to a Nightingale":
>   Still wouldst thou sing, and I have ears in vain—
>   To thy high requiem become a sod.

"The Eve of St Agnes":
>   She clos'd the door, she panted, all akin
>   To spirits of the air, and visions wide:
>   No uttered syllable, or, woe betide!

But to her heart, her heart was voluble,
Paining with eloquence her balmy side;
As though a tongueless nightingale should swell
Her throat in vain, and die, heart-stifled, in her dell.

"La Belle Dame Sans Merci"
    and no birds sing

I am most interested in his Philomela reference in "The
Eve of St. Agnes." It is not only that his Madeline is like
Philomela, voiceless while her body throbs with unspoken
pain, but that Keats' Philomela, his nightingale, must die.

*   *   *

DEMETRIUS
So, now go tell, an if thy tongue can speak,
Who 'twas that cut thy tongue and ravish'd thee.

CHIRON
Write down thy mind, bewray thy meaning so,
An if thy stumps will let thee play the scribe.

~~DEMETRIUS~~

~~She hath no tongue to call, nor hands to wash;~~
~~And so let's leave her to her silent walks.~~

*   *   *

Is the metonym, finally, for Philomela art, or silence, or raving? Later poets' use of the nightingale suggests she is a poet able to sing about and against suffering, but Ovid never mentions song. Instead, he symbolizes Philomela and Procne by their murder of Itys: "And even so the red marks of the murder/ stayed on their breasts; the feathers were blood-colored." What is our longing to hear Philomela's song but our own desire for retributive justice? Ovid's story is clear: the tongue which might give voice to reparation is mute beside the body's recounting of injury. Philomela's story, then, is meant to excite, to enrage.

—*The Metamorphoses*, 6.672–673

*   *   *

Perhaps the greatest desire a victim of violence has is to look, in memory, at that violence dispassionately. But remembering, the heart pounds, the body floods with adrenaline, ready to tear back off into flight. For some, there is no smoothing chaos into memory. Poetry, with its suggestion that time and pain can be ordered through language, strains to constrain suffering. It suggests, but rarely achieves, the redress we desire. Language does not heal terror, and if it brings us closer to imagining the sufferer's experience, this too does not necessarily make us feel greater compassion, but a desire for further sensation. If we cannot articulate pain beyond inspiring in the listener a need for revenge, we speak only of and to the body.

*   *   *

Philomela's first communication of pain is visual: like a film, her tortures scroll action by action across her tapestry. Like a film, these images manipulate emotion: Philomela's pain cannot be relieved except through equivalent, mimetic actions that heighten the need for, but never achieve, the catharsis denied the original sufferer.

*   *   *

What if it is the form, not the content, of *The Metamorphoses* that is the terror? Each story unfolding into another, perpetually disrupting, thus delaying the ending? What if, because we came to listen, we are the reason the story keeps not ending? Why should Philomela ever sing, when our presence only increases her suffering?

*   *   *

Sufferance: ME *soffrance* and Latin *suffrer,* patient endurance; the suffering of pain, trouble, damage, wrong; sanction, consent or acquiescence.

   Suffer: to cause pain; also, to endure pain.

*   *   *

That the branches of poetry are silence and sufferance.

*   *   *

In my poem, "Philomela," the woman who has been raped inherits—years after her attack—an antique sewing machine from her grandmother. She imagines using this machine to sew a quilt on which she will embroider figures of the domestic life her grandmother ruefully noted she did not have: a house, a child, a man. But after a few minutes' contemplation, she boxes up the machine, slides it high up on a bedroom shelf. What is she communicating? Who would she be speaking to? She can always return to the quilt, she tells herself, but in the unwritten rest of the poem I imagine for her, she never will.

*   *   *

Not rape, I say, meaning certain body parts and not others were used, meaning I do not cede that last ignominy to him, will never name how I lay in the dirt and ground my screams back down into me. But what is the word for what I experienced after? What is the word for how I awoke to fear and never went back to sleep?

*   *   *

Time drives the flocks from field to fold,
When Rivers rage and Rocks grow cold,

And Philomel becometh dumb,
The rest complains of cares to come—

At some point, the nightingale falls silent. Time erases
the song by numbing the wound, replacing it with fresh
complaints: new hurts the singer can't yet fathom.

 —Sir Walter Ralegh, "The Nymph's Reply to the
  Shepherd," 5-8

* * *

I'd like to imagine the fact I fought was the reason
the attack ended, but the truth is he let me go. If he'd
wanted more, there was no question *more* would have
happened. I would have stopped fighting and become
what some might call an accomplice to the act. I was, in
fact, already going limp, subtly acceding to his desires
in the hopes that, having satisfied them, he would stop.
Perhaps this is why he pushed himself away. Perhaps it
was enough that he'd grabbed and inserted and taken
what he could within narrow legal, or personal, limits to
prove a point to me and to himself: anything he wanted
he could have. In the end, I was not so much a body to

be reckoned with but a structure he would humiliate and dismantle.

*   *   *

In life, time's passage allows us to see ourselves change, but a poem's chronology forces us to see repetition: lyric time is not progressive but fragmentary and recursive. Traumatic time works like lyric time: the *now* of terror repeatedly breaking back through the crust of one's consciousness. Mourning the wound thus becomes an obsessive love of the lost. Mourning is merely the process by which we remain frozen: the birds always in flight, the hoopoe continually in pursuit. O, could our mourning ease thy misery!

    —*Titus Andronicus,* II, iv

*   *   *

One fantasy, in and outside of poetry, is that time itself stops. But Ralegh's point is that time never stops. Instead, its continual unfolding disorders memory, it blunts and numbs. Time is the subject that finally silences Philomela.

*   *   *

Compassion and retributive justice require that we hold multiple senses of time alive in mind: the past event, a punishment's present, the future in which this crime cannot or will no longer be enacted. Compassion calls for complex responses where vengeance calls for only one: a raving.

I don't have compassion for my attacker, just as I don't have a word for that day, only a description of its unfolding. Behind these descriptions, you may imagine the word or punishment you think appropriate. This act is done for yourself. It is not, though you may believe it is, at all useful to me.

*   *   *

Lucky, I think after he leaves, my shirt torn, nose running. Nothing stirs in the woods. Still I sit on the forest floor, unsure where to run. Will he come back? Will he be on the trail, will I see him in town? At the thought of town, at the thought of being seen by him or any other human, I shake and burn with shame.

*   *   *

I suspect it helped, not knowing what to call what happened in the woods. Not having the word, or refusing a word, forced me to imagine my own, allowed me both the privacy of my grief and the invention of private rituals to heal this grief. Keeping my attack secret also shielded me from the very real possibility of being called a hysteric. In that sense, silence protected me. Would I have grieved differently if someone had given me a legal term, a support group, a brochure?

Over time, shame and rage have abated. But not the memory. And not, at times, the overwhelming certainty that one day soon I will not be lucky again.

*   *   *

The nightingale hovers between trauma and memory, its song meant to bring one into concert with the other, to integrate event into narrative, to bring pain out of the body and into language. But the song isn't heard, it's longed for. "Heard melodies are sweet," Keats writes, "but those unheard/ are sweeter." The healing voice of the nightingale is only beautiful when lodged in the imagination ("Jug jug," Eliot croons). The song stops, the nightingale dies, and once more, we descend into silence.

> —Keats, "Ode on a Grecian Urn," 11-12
> —T. S. Eliot, "The Waste Land," II, 27

*   *   *

Sappho saw the nightingale as a messenger of springtime and renewal. Pliny the Elder said the bird could sing more than one song; nightingales engage in singing contests, their songs changing over time. The song, then, is not generic, but individualized, depending on the hour of day and also on the season. In poetry, the song may be one of suffering and loss; in nature, it is simply one of life.

> —Pliny the Elder, *Historia Naturalis*, Book 10,
>   Chapter 43

*   *   *

Does the bird sing or does it not sing? Is it a symbol for what threatens to overwhelm our senses, or for what permanently transforms? The bird is death. No wonder Keats imagines himself dying when he hears it. No wonder he scratches out the speech of Lavinia's tormentors in his copy of Shakespeare: silence will come for him, as well as for her, and for all of us. There is no shame in it. Death attends our longing for the song. Sing, for you are voiceless. Sing, for it cannot matter. Sing, for soon no one will hear you again.

*   *   *

I have spent my life devoted to an art whose foundational symbol is one of unspeakable violence. Did I seek poetry out for this? Or was I, that day in the woods, made into a poet? Perhaps, whether we are changed into our opposites or shrunk into the form that best defines us, some part of transformation is always a curse. *I am what I always was.* Perhaps it is sentimental to suggest violence has given me meaning, that the heart of poetry was ever and only silence. Madness to say, yes, there's pain, but would I have changed without it?

*   *   *

If the song is beautiful, you will listen. In the field one day outside the residency, I encounter, or think I encounter, the bird that's charmed the opera singer. I am near a row of acacia trees when I hear its sudden, piercing trill of notes rise and fall. It could be any kind of bird, really, any kind of song. A cry of sex or terror, a mimicry of its parents or an invention all its own. A flourish it will teach to its offspring, its own embellishments branching through the ancient notes. It is the sound of time. It is the sound of time passing.

*   *   *

I stand in the field. I whistle back.

LETTER TO MYSELF UPON ENTERING COLLEGE

BY CAITLIN DONOHUE

DEAR CAITLIN,

Congratulations on getting into college! What a privilege. Not to say you didn't do your part to make it here. (High school yearbooks don't edit themselves!) Many good and many terrible things will happen to you on this well-pruned, high-fenced campus. Keep in mind that the most disturbing and bewildering moments will make you— me!—a stronger Older Caitlin.

Let's not spend too much time discussing academics. You'll do just fine. So much reading awaits you, a bibliophile's dream. Your sociology courses will impart a necessary anger towards society's inequities, and you'll find much to rage against outside the classroom as well. You, my West Coast public school–raised duckling, should earn study-abroad credit for navigating the social waters of an all-but-Ivy-League pond of wealthy, New England boarding school alums. Your year in Madrid will be less of a culture shock.

I know you're currently eying the legacy students and considering converting to their aesthetic. Don't waste your time. Pink and green don't pair. Salmon-red pants and those tiny embroidered elephants are atrocities. Stick to your initial reaction: no one should get to wear such '80s-throwback frivolities without being pickpocketed. Besides, your true uniform will develop soon enough: more dog collars than pearl necklaces, a show of allegiance to the worldwide queer mafia rather than to someone's grandparents' country club.

Any minute now you'll hear about a party at one of the oldest frats on campus—founded in 1850! Designated a national historic landmark in 1985! The party will be called "Anything for Money." This is how your classmates will meet their future spouses, but no house in the Hamptons awaits you for starring in some rich boy's *Girls Gone Wild*–style cell phone video. Stay in and study your sociology.

There will be incidents during these years that I won't make light of in this letter. You are entering a four-year struggle to maintain bodily autonomy. There will be young men who kiss you roughly before you decide whether you want them to. There will be times when you wake up in bed with a near-stranger. It will be easy to tell yourself on these mornings that Everclear punch and a healthy sex drive are to blame. This may be true. But there will also be the male "friend" who sneaks into your bed at night when you're passed out, drunk and naked and ever so trusting of the sanctity of your bedroom. He will act bewildered when you scream at him to leave. Neither of you will mention the incident again.

Your girlfriends will prove to be little help in maintaining your sanity in the face of such things. Be easy on these women. They live on this campus too.

The embarrassment and self-doubt born on campus will never leave you. But they will form a shade in the palette you'll go on to use as a professional writer, a heavy matte gray that contrasts with the bright, beautiful colors of your many friends, your many triumphs. In time you will count among your loved ones drag queens and porn stars and intellectuals, and, most beloved of all, people who are all three. You will host parties in heels and lashes and bustiers, your queenliness under a spotlight. You will get regular STD checkups. You will have dates who teach you that gender roles are a lie used by capitalism to herd sheep. You will live to see an age in which the exposure of bad men doing bad things is popular enough to be dismissed as a trend by threatened patriarchs. You will learn that sexual desire can generate not just cruelty and discomfort, but also strength and community.

You will break your chronic attraction to flippant men who have no business holding your breasts, much less your heart. You will learn from queer friends a sense of self that you will wish had been available to you on those mornings-after when you avoided the waffle iron in the cafeteria because it left your back exposed to the jock tables for too long. Years later, though, prepping for your close-up, you will remember when you wanted to be invisible, and you will laugh into your makeup mirror, apply another layer of eyeliner, and film your first sex scene.

Maintain your exercise regime and eat complete meals. Keep hold of your physical form. It is tangible proof of that which they say is theirs and must never be. This body— this untanned, traveling, designer clothes-free body—you must hang onto it and love it during these tough years. In the squalid, square lethargy of your dorm room you cannot even imagine its future glory.

In the meantime, feel easy but keep your distance from these man-children, these beautiful starved women. Buy a sippy cup, glue jewels on it, and bring it to frat parties. Gesture to it with a big smile when someone offers you a drink, and make a practice of holding onto the handle when they pour you a cocktail. Never the punch.

I repeat, C, congratulations! These battlefield years will whittle you into a strong woman. The cuts you receive will enable you to recognize the wounds of others. You are special, you are loved, you are yours.

Believe it,
Older Caitlin

LINGER

BY GABRIELLE BELLOT

WHEN I WAS A TEENAGER, my uncle began to smile at me in a strange, lingering way. He was the ex-husband of an auntie who often came to our house in Dominica to have tea and chat with my mother, and because he had a name going back generations on our island and owned a prominent IGA supermarket in the capital, just about everyone knew who he was. He was average height with a rounded head, short whitening hair, brown freckles against a red-white complexion, a trimmed graying mustache, and a boyish, toothy smile. With his loose polo shirts, slacks, and oxfords, he looked nothing so much as like a British colonial from before the days of our independence. He talked cricket scores avidly. Whenever he saw me he would grin and chant juvenile malapropisms of mine, like *lopper* for *lobster*.

I hadn't as yet come out as transgender, didn't fully understand what it meant to see a girl reflected in my mind's mirror, and because I feared people seeing that inner girl I acted macho to throw everyone off my trail. But when I began to sense something in my uncle's relationship with me had shifted, I wondered, if he, too, had glimpsed her. I wondered if she was a kind of dim lighthouse beam to him.

One evening, he came to congratulate me for getting into graduate school in Florida. My father had grown up without the means to go to college, so he had worked assiduously to win the coveted island scholarship that allowed him to go to university in Jamaica and, later, medical school in the United States. That I was also aiming to become a doctor, if one of philosophy (like my mum), was cause for familial merriment.

My uncle smiled at me. We should celebrate, he told me in private, just me and him. There would be red wine, he said—and, he added, voice whisper-slurring, a tub. A special party, just for you and me, with water and wine.

The way he said it startled and discomfited me. But I was young and silly and trusting, imagining that safety and goodness simply orbited around the cheery sun of my uncle, so I just smiled back. *Sure, if we have time.*

His lingering smile, again.

I knew something was off, but I didn't want to believe it. He was my kind, jocular, generous uncle; how could he be asking me to be intimate with him? In my naïveté, I decided I had read too much into it and resolved to put it out of my mind, though a peculiar, perverse image of us in a tub, fragrant with rose petals, sharing glasses of red wine, stayed with me.

A few years passed. The unsettling scene never had a chance to play out, partly because my graduate work kept me in Florida. I almost forgot about the exchange altogether—until a return visit to Dominica. At a holiday party thrown by my uncle—a party I thought would be like any other family festivity—he rekindled and proved my suspicions.

The event was primarily my aunties, uncles, and a few cousins; I may have been the youngest there. The green-dark evening was warm and loud with the Bartókian night-music of desirous insects and the calls of frogs drawn by the earlier rains, and if you listened carefully you would hear the occasional distant report of a bamboo cannon somewhere in the mountains.

As the evening lengthened, my uncle drank and caroused with the other partygoers, but I found his gaze alighting on me every so often. I recognized the look and wondered if he was sailing on a gondola down a long-forbidden canal, waiting for his chance to dock next to me.

Eventually, he sat down beside me. His thigh touched mine; his pants were crisp and cool. He whispered, almost in a growl, *You're real sexy*. He said he wanted me. Said it more than once. I didn't know how to respond. I was terrified. All I knew was that I couldn't say anything to anyone else. I was afraid no one would believe me, that mentioning it would somehow out me as queer even though I had not reciprocated. I was afraid, even, that saying *no* might hurt my uncle.

His thigh, warming the fabric, moved against mine. I thanked him for the compliment, not knowing what else to say. We could do something, he murmured. I said I didn't know, stood, and backed into the living room. He followed me to a sofa. My mother, smiling obliviously, sat next to me just as he was about to sit, putting a barrier between him and me. He got furious and began asking, gutturally, why she was there. He tried to push her off. Like everyone else, my mother presumed he was just belligerent from intoxication. I clung near her for the rest of the night, afraid to be alone with my uncle, who went on to drink so precipitously that he eventually needed to be held up by two other men. He grinned boyishly all the while, though his eyes also held a defeated sadness.

For years, I said nothing. I came out as transgender, which, due to my island's anti-queer atmosphere, made returning home unfeasible. My mother could not accept my transition; my father offered support, but even he insisted that I not return. They came, occasionally, to see me in America instead.

Over breakfast one morning on a Christmas trip to the French Quarter of New Orleans, I finally told my father about my uncle. My mum had just stormed off in fury after informing me, yet again, that I had disgraced her by coming out and that, perhaps, if my father had played more sports with me, I might have turned out "right." In the tempest wake of her indignation, I was nervous; I didn't want to add to his stress. To my surprise, he took it in calm stride. All that seemed to matter to him was that I was okay. I'm not sure I was, but I felt better telling him.

I already knew I couldn't return home and hope for any semblance of happiness or normalcy as an out queer woman. After mulling over what had happened with my uncle, I understood another reason I was grateful not to return: I wouldn't have to face him. I had loved his avuncular kindness for so long; now, he casts a shadow that scares me.

I don't know if I could face him today. Don't know if I could forgive and be comfortable in his presence again, even as I want to believe I can forgive and re-embrace anyone.

After coming out, I began to feel it everywhere from men: a devouring gaze, a hunger. And I learned, too, that many men refused to take *no* for an answer.

A guy I met through OKCupid in Florida probably hurt me the most. He was the second man I had ever gone out with. I've always preferred being with other women romantically—most of my daydreams from my youth were of me as a girl with another girl at my side—and so I had little romantic or sexual experience with men. They seemed almost new to me, *terra incognita*.

I was naïve, so I let him take me, on our first and only date, to his place, a ramshackle gray house in a part of town I wasn't familiar with. The place was malodorous with the scent of weed. His roommate offered us some. My tolerance was low, but I took the bong. In a few moments, I felt like I was in an oceanic fog, almost drunk. I panicked. I knew pot was generally safe, but I had never taken so strong a strain. He put his hand on my leg and smiled at me in that lingering way. After a while, he led me upstairs.

I was so out of it that I almost passed out on his bed. Making an effort to wake up, I rose and we began to kiss. I told him I was okay with anything except using a certain part of my body.

When we were naked, he suddenly grabbed that part of me. *No*, I said. *Stop.*

He went down on me. I felt detached, disoriented, as if it were happening from a distance. I told him no. He kept going. I pleaded for him to stop.

He paused. I asked if he understood why it discomforted me as a trans woman, why I couldn't accept him touching me there. He shrugged and went back down on me. I didn't know if his roommate knew I was trans, so I was afraid of alerting him if I screamed, afraid it might lead to some greater violence than the one already happening to me. Finally, I yelled. The guy stopped. I was shaking, but he'd left me terrified.

I wondered, as he drove me home, what would have happened if he had become belligerent when I asked him to cease.

I was learning, again, the limits of *no*.

It became routine to expect men to ask for sex and to keep after me even after I said *no*. Security guards in museums propositioned me. In Queens, a man saw me kissing my girlfriend on a sidewalk and repeatedly asked us how much it would cost to hire us as prostitutes. A taxi driver in Tallahassee told me over and over not to leave his car because I was beautiful; after I asked for the fifth or sixth time to be let me out of the cab, he gave me his card, told me to call him, and stood silently beside his car, watching me walk up to my apartment. I feared he would follow me. I listened for his knock, for the rattling of a lock.

It took years to realize how much I was letting men get away with—the stares, the catcalls, the fear of pounding on my door from men who had followed, hunted me to my home—because I had let such toxic behavior become, as Hannah Arendt said of evil, banal.

For a long time, I brushed it under the rug, minimized it all. To be honest, I was afraid of speaking out. I had read too many stories of trans women who went to the police after men harassed them and were told by the cops that it was the trans women's own fault; what do you expect, the officers asked, when you dress like a woman? It was a version of blaming the victims of assault for how they dress, but now mixed with a sense that we, as trans women, were asking for trouble by presenting as female. We were to blame, it seemed, first for being women, then for being the wrong kind of women. I came to feel ashamed, at times, of what I was, stupidly believing, even as I should have known better, that my stories didn't matter because I wasn't the right kind of woman.

This cuts to the core of how I feel about the #MeToo movement—that I both do and don't fit. As a trans woman,

I find the movement engendered by #MeToo both affirming and isolating. It's helped me see that I should never excuse harassment as "not that bad." Yet the movement, well-intentioned as it is, it rarely seems nuanced enough to include someone like me. Anti-abuse rhetoric tends toward a categorical oversimplification, attacking all people with penises as rapacious rapists—which leaves pre-op trans women, including those who would otherwise sympathize with many cis women's harrowing experiences of harassment, in an uncomfortable position.

What heals, I've come to learn, is faith in the power of other women, faith in an open-armed sisterhood and in talking openly—especially about how my experiences both intersect with and deviate from those of most cis women. From this, I have begun to learn again how to trust, even if the fear never fully leaves that any man can suddenly begin to cast a new, more terrible shadow.

Speaking lights a candle in a room inside us.

MY BODY,
MY STORY

BY KARISSA CHEN

THERE IS A STORY that lives inside my body. My body does not lie. We say *listen to your gut*, but I have learned to listen with my liver, my lungs, my back, my sternum, my palms, my teeth. I have left men because their gaslighting left my jaw sore; I have imagined my beloved's departure and read love in the twinge in my chest. I have felt guilt trapped in the cold sweat on my spine, security in the bright light expanding in my lungs after laughter. Sometimes my body tells me things whether I want to know them or not. Sometimes it keeps secrets from me, burying them until the day I crack a memory open. That's when my body surprises.

For years I told this story with laughter: deep in throes of depression, caught in an unhealthy relationship with X, a man who was lying to me, I met up with a different man, Y, an old friend, for drinks. Both of us temporarily back in the city we had moved away from, the city where X lived. I'd tell how we got drunk, bought condoms, booked a hotel room, tried to have sex, could not have sex because he was too drunk to maintain an erection. How, exhausted, the alcohol wearing us down, we tumbled over into sleep. *I awoke to him on top of me!* I'd laugh to friends, at the big surprise turn of the story. *Already fucking me!* How I saw my phone on the bedside table and began to text X behind Y's back. *Literally behind his back!* I'd say, delighted. *He was so drunk he didn't even notice.* This was the punchline of the story, the hilarious image of a man drunkenly thrusting and grunting against me, oblivious as I indifferently texted someone else. *How crazy is that?* And then the finale: how, when X asked to see me, I pushed Y off my body and locked myself in the bathroom, calling X before running back out to pull on my clothes. How I fled the hotel room with incoherent apologies, leaving behind a gold bracelet I loved.

The worst thing, I'd say, *was leaving that bracelet behind, all for a horrible one-night stand!*

As I grew older, my understanding of consent evolved and so did the vocabulary I used to describe this incident. *Hilarious story* turned to *gray area* to *assault* to *rape*. Even after I came to the realization that I'd indeed experienced a form of assault, I recited the statement as fact, not as lived bodily experience. *It sucked but I'm not traumatized*, I maintained. *Maybe it barely qualifies as assault*.

What I forgot, for years and years, were the details of what my body experienced at the time. But my body did not forget.

I'd been trying to write this story down for this essay for weeks, but I kept finding excuses not to. Work I had to do, movies I had to see, long chats with friends who needed my advice. With the deadline looming, I tried to write a pared-down third-person version, a narrator like a hovering eye. I failed. Finally I braved a first-person, linear, confessional account. *I've told this story before. I just have to tell it with a little bit more honesty*.

How hard can it be?

It was in the process of trying to be *accurate* that I became aware, with alarm and surprise, of the nausea mounting in my gut, of the way my throat was closing up, of how suddenly I felt like I could not breathe and yet I might vomit if I tried to save myself from asphyxiation. I feel this now, at the very moment I am typing this. Each key is difficult to press. Each word results in a throb, a pulse against the insides of my chest, my throat, my eyelids.

I remember now: the sudden confusion of waking to pressure, the gray light filtering through the windows, the disorientation. The pain of it, the rough stickiness of dry skin being peeled and chafed, the fisted meat shoving itself through me. The numb realization that he was not wearing a condom. His closed eyes hanging above mine, his morning breath hot against my skin. The turn of my head to look at something else, anything else, because I felt I had no right to say *no*. The clamminess of my palm wrapping around my phone. The stupefaction at the understanding that at that moment I was so little of a *person* to Y that he had not even noticed. The relief to find that X—whom I both loved and hated—had texted. The irrational flood of salvation worming through me. The cold bathroom tile shocking my bare butt as I huddled and dialed his number. The chilly November dawn outside the hotel.

And later: the bruises on my thighs. The soreness of my crotch. The dirty linoleum of the Walgreens floor where I crouched as I confessed to X what had happened. The two hours I huddled in X's shower, crying. The two days of diarrhea I suffered after that, apropos of nothing. The humiliation I thought the doctor could see when I went in for STD testing. The way I hated my body for weeks, wanting to claw off my own skin with my nails or sandpaper or razors.

I had forgotten all of this because I'd told no one about it for years—no one except X, who, despite all of his assholery, stilled my hands that day and insisted I was not dirty or disgusting or deserving of everything that had happened. And so time passed, and I survived—the rape, the depression, the terrible relationship with X—and the narrative changed in my mind and I forgot. Until now.

I am not interested, now, in pointing fingers or burning Y's life down. For better or for worse, I feel absolutely nothing towards him. What I am interested in is my body. The memory that lives in my body. My body that cannot lie. It is a body that has so often been out of my control. A body that our culture told Y was his for the taking, even in my sleep. It is a body that is legislated by men who have never met me. A body society feels it has a right to shame, to put standards upon, to comment on. A body disrespected by men who have taken from me both consensually and non-consensually. A body cherished, enjoyed, cared for by men who have loved me. It is a body that has laughed and ached and danced and a body that I have sometimes sought to destroy, especially during the period of my life when I thought I deserved every bad thing that came my way. It is a body that often reaches for fight or flight, a body my therapist has determined has rewired itself due to PTSD. It is a body whose womb hopes to one day carry a child, a body that grows lean and certain from daily runs, a body that knows my craving for good food is the surest sign that I am happy. It is a body that has not forgotten what it has survived, even if I want to tell another story.

A week after the incident, Y emailed me and said he had my bracelet. I asked him to mail it to me, but he kept forgetting. Months later, we both knew we would be at a friend's birthday party. When I arrived, he was standing outside the bar, smoking. Without a word, he reached into his pocket with his free hand and gave me my bracelet.

Thank you, I said, smiling awkwardly. I did not hug him. For years I wore that bracelet with various outfits, relieved to have it back in my possession. In retrospect, I think I felt it was a token of what I did not lose that morning.

And now I wait to see if telling this story, if putting it into words made permanent by ink and paper, will help exorcise the symptoms rushing through my body. I wait to see if this is how we begin to heal our bodies, by airing out what we have forced them to reckon with silently, protectively, alone.

RE: YOUR
RAPE STORY

BY ELISSA SCHAPPELL

FROM: LAUREN
TO: KATE
MONDAY, 4 P.M.

HEY KATE,

First, I have to say, I love this piece so much!!! If it were up to me, I wouldn't touch a word. But there are a few little things, questions mostly, totally on me, I'm sure I wasn't clear at lunch. It was that Condé Nast special—rare burger, no bun, no fries, no fun, and two just-kill-me sodas. Ouch!

Anyway, it was so great talking to you. You were so honest—or maybe it was the tequila talking? (But wait, I don't speak Spanish! lol.) Which is why I have to say, I'm a little surprised [and a tad bit disappointed] that a lot of the great stuff you told me isn't in here, because I felt like we really connected.

And how crazy that you grew up just one town over! Some of my friends had older sisters and brothers so it's totally possible we were at some of the same parties. Small world!

Actually, I used to babysit for a family in your town, maybe you knew them.

Okay—let's jump right in. I know this deadline is INSANE and I'm sorry, but let me say again how thrilled I am that you're doing this.

What would you think about rewriting the opening? You get it right? Stats are a total nonstarter. We all know the number of sexual assaults, rapes, nonreported rapes that occur every year is HUGE (omg that Mount Everest of untested rape kits—soooo grim), and that's the problem, the numbers are so mind-boggling you can't even wrap your head around them.

It's incredible. For centuries women don't want to talk about rape because they're afraid of being punished, shamed, or having no one believe them, and then one day Harvey Weinstein comes along, drops his bathrobe and boom! It's like magic. Suddenly everybody has their hand up, Me too! Me too! And a movement is born! Did you see the piece in the NYT about Boomer moms being triggered by classic rock in shopping malls, and what about that little old lady who was goosed by a porter on the Titanic?

So many...

You have to wonder if some women aren't voting twice, jk!

No listen. If I could write this piece I would, in a heartbeat. The exposure you're going to get!!! Not that you need it, or care, Ms. Army of 2 million Twitter followers. This will be easy money for you. (I know that money is a thing for you right now.) Just tell us what happened to you, and how you got past it. I am not saying the ending has to be uplifting, but you know.

Don't hate me but I need this ASAP, like our real drop-dead deadline is next Friday.

FYI I wanted to do #MeToo months ago, but the editor in chief (you know him, right?) wouldn't do it, swore it was a fad, it would never last. Did I mention that we've started calling him Oz? As in Wizard of... because he wants to have a hand in everything, total control, unless of course he's mysteriously disappeared to go hot-air ballooning.

Now he's freaking out that by the time the issue hits the stands #MeToo will be dead (like he's been predicting for months), and it will be all about the #Backlash.

He is determined to be ahead of the curve on #Backlash. Seriously, we're about to have our first meeting, I can't tell you the number of times he's said, joking/not joking, "One day this is going to come back and bite women on the ass."

All my best,
L

P.S. Attaching that hilarious pic I told you about of the entire editorial staff in our pink pussy hats.

MONDAY, 5:30 P.M.

Oops, spaced on the contract. (If I only had a brain, a heart, some courage...) Sending ASAP and YES we do pay on acceptance not publication. I can expedite if you like. Sisterhood is powerful. Yay us!

WEDNESDAY, 3:33 P.M.

Dear Katie,

Oh my god, Please believe me, I didn't mean to rewrite you! You have to believe me, It's your story not mine. 100% yours.

I only revised that party scene so you'd get an idea of the kinda world-building details we want. See, I didn't know if you were in college or high school. If it was one guy or two guys, and I don't know how drunk/stoned you were. What happened? If you told me at lunch I blacked it out. Do you think maybe someone slipped you a roofie?

Is it possible this could be a teachable moment?

I could have sworn you told me that you woke up with your underwear on backward. It sounds here like maybe you lost it? Forgot it? Clarify.

I know this is dumb, but what were you wearing? Ugh. I know, but the reader will wonder and it will help them better imagine the scene.

Also, did you report? That will be important to readers. Did you report? And no judgment if you didn't!

I'd say that publishing your story would more than make up for it.

As a fellow English major, I appreciate that you're trying

to conjure a mood with that "heavy canopy of smoke over the dance floor," but how about just "smoky"? Not so sure about details like "The slow oscillation of a fan moving the air like hands"? Or the motif of the red camp blanket with the print of hunters and the hound dogs on it. Worship all of it but in the interest of space we will have to lose some of it. I want to hear the throbbing bass of the stereo, smell that smoke—is it pot, hashish??

On another note, Amen to your comment about those privileged "ivory tower feminists with their Harvard degrees and peashooters" attacking women who complain about sexual assault, *Grow up!* and *Stop whining!*

I mean, what would THEY do if their boss exposed himself in the break room while they were trying to microwave Cup o' Noodles? Quit? Slap him with a lawsuit? Slap him? What if he appeared out of nowhere and said it was an accident? Would it matter whether or not you were eating?

Love that you included that taxi ride with the "boy genius" editor (boy genius leaning back hard into his forties) who passed on your book because you wouldn't let him grope you in the taxi. That line "your cunt is made of ice, frozen and impenetrable as Superman's Fortress of Solitude" is priceless. Kudos to you for saying what no one else will, but unfortunately, we can't use it even with ***s. It's silly but the magazine doesn't allow offensive language or profanity, even in dialogue.

Re: money. I promise I'm trying to get you $2 a word (times are tough but you deserve it)! You're an established writer and a vocal feminist, and what a great platform this is for you, right? Just get the piece in—seriously knock it out of the effing park and cross my heart I'll get you $2.

Also, Oz says feminists have no sense of humor. Maybe you could make this a little funny? Add a few jokes? It might soften him up...

Yours in the struggle,
L

P.S. I think the pussy hat pic is cute too.

P.P.S. Just sign the contract. Once the piece comes in—and he loves it—we'll change it from $1 to $2.

P.P.P.S. Mea culpa, I know that joke about women "voting twice" was dumb.

FRIDAY, 5:30 P.M.

Hello friend,

Good news, I'm still at the office! I get that you're stressed. I wasn't suggesting you "throw in some rape jokes." I would never do that. I was suggesting maybe you could lighten the mood, that's all, if it wouldn't kill you but clearly you think it's a bad idea.

L

FRIDAY, 6:00 P.M.

Can I give you some advice? In times like this I always return to the master: Charles Dickens. Dickens says if you want to hook the reader and gain their sympathy you have to tell them a story. I'm not saying you're Oliver Twist or David Copperfield, but ask yourself, because the reader wants to know: *Are you or are you not the hero of your own story?*

Screw nuance. It's black-and-white. No gray. Gray is for foreign movies with subtitles. You know, woman smoking a cigarette weeps silently at the sight of a bicycle with a flat tire.

Think about it. Anyway, hope this all makes sense. I am happy to talk it through with you. Sorry about the misunderstanding.

Also we should have some art soon, very excited to run it by you!

Yours in Solidarity!

P.S. You got this. Forget about getting that emergency root canal, sister. If you give us the kind of searing realism that gets people talking, Oz will buy you a fur coat. LOL. We will definitely go out and get white girl wasted.

MONDAY, 10:45 A.M.

Yes, confirmed. I got the contract.

Sigh. I see you stetted that "some women, some women" section. I know every woman experiences sexual harassment/sexual assault/rape differently. I know that "it's personal," it's supposed to be a personal piece. Remember? That's what we agreed on.

So, get personal. Get right to that "elbow-titting" thing those guys did in the halls of your high school. THAT'S

GREAT. How did they get away with that? No, I know. It's that *You-should-be-happy-he-hit-you-it-means-he-likes-you* thing, am I right? I hate that. Also LOVE the image of trying to dodge the ass-grabbing customers in that beach restaurant being like a game of Whac-A-Mole, the minute you escape one hairy varmint another pops up.

This is what I mean about funny!!! Maybe more humor would be good?

Someone joked the other day that girls who like male attention should wear a cute little button, like a wink emoji or *Flirting Zone*, to signal that they're safe to talk to, compliment, hang out with, etc....

Here's a crazy idea, maybe we should look at this from a service angle? Provide a sort of a visual, a chart (maybe in the shape of dress?) laying out what's generally considered acceptable behavior and what's sexual harassment/sexual assault/rape—not from the point of view of the law, but from a woman's point of view.

Since you're wed to the "not all women experience sexual harassment the same way" thing, the headline could be something like "Jane says bad behavior, Sally says sexual violation." Keep it snappy.

At one end you've got the 100-year-old grandfather

who pats you on the fanny and says, *Va va va voom*, then whistling construction workers, then strangers looking down your shirt on the bus, followed by coworkers who say, "If I told you that you had a nice body would you hold it against me?" or coworkers who sometimes rub your shoulders, then all the other stuff, you know, groping, date rape, all the way to being raped at knifepoint.

How's that?

Question: Where on this scale would you put the father who every Saturday night, before he takes the babysitter home, parks his car around the corner from her house so he can feel her up? All through middle school.

I can't write it for you, you'd have to figure it out.

Best,
XOXOXO

Hey, did you get my last email?? Are your ears burning?

They should be. We had our first #MeTooBacklash meeting yesterday and your name came up! Oz was not joking about being ahead of the pack here. He also asked me again when he could see your piece. There's a lot of buzz about it here... I am stalling, but I can't hold him off much longer. He said, "I want details," I said he'd have to wait. But seriously, tick tock tick tock. We are running out of time.

We looked at possible cover art for #MeTooBacklash. Hey, can I run something past you? I know you've got a great eye. What would you think about either a woman in a neck brace, like "whiplash," or a woman on a hill waving a white flag in surrender—and the white flag is a white miniskirt? Maybe off-base, just running it up the old flagpole.

(ha ha wink emoji)

Can't wait to get your reaction to the attached art for your story.

Ugh... I do have some bad news. I'm sorry and I hate this so much, but zero percent chance we'd publish this without your name on it. No initials, no pseudonym. That's the whole point. It's you. Also zero percent chance for a kill fee now after all this.

But hey, let's be positive! Ask yourself, WWGSD? What Would Gloria Steinem Do? Sisterhood is powerful!

Cheers!
XO

TUESDAY, 10:05 A.M.

Wow! Rise and shine girlfriend. *Were you really up at 4 a.m.?*

I am going to pretend you didn't just send this back to me—again—without directly addressing my questions. I am going to pretend this didn't happen.

Also, what about the chart we talked about? Grand-father, construction worker, knifepoint, babysitter being molested in the driveway?

Relax. I spoke to the art department about swapping out the image of Raggedy Ann in the mouth of the dog "wolf" and they're fine with it. Who knows where that image even came from, but you have to admit it's arresting. It catches the eye. Danger!

Tell me the truth—is it the photo, or do you have a problem with Raggedy Ann personally? Personally, I love Raggedy Ann. I mean she's the all-American "Every Girl" doll, right? Didn't you have one?

Honestly, we're all a little surprised at how upset you are by this image. Outside of Raggedy Ann being in a dog's mouth no one here thinks she looks like "the victim of a violent assault," or "traumatized... like she's just going through the motions... putting on a happy face for her friends and family." I don't see how button eyes can project a "haunted stare," but what matters is you do. You see "a mask of pain," I see a poker face—and if she is putting on a happy face, is that the worst thing?

Don't forget she's smiling! :) You can't deny that big smile. Raggedy Ann is no one's chew toy. Hell, I can think of a dozen photos of me where I am smiling like that. Of course I'm drunk, and she's not, *she's a doll*, but what matters is she/we are having fun. I think that's the point. Even in the jaws of a dog Raggedy Ann continues to smile, she never loses her sense of humor.

Jean-Claude Phillipe, you know our art director, yes? He says what else could it be but a reference to Little Red Riding Hood and the Big Bad Wolf? Is the wolf not the epitome of stranger danger? *Danger!*

They also say if the issue is the saliva, they can lose it.

For the record, nobody here interpreted this as crying wolf = crying rape.

L

WEDNESDAY, 10:10 A.M.

Dearest Katie,

I just want you to know that of course, the minute you said that, I saw it. I don't know how I missed it. Crying wolf. At this point I think I'm too close to this piece. I literally broke down crying twice yesterday. I had a dream that I was back in middle school and my mom and dad, and the mom and the kids I used to babysit for (but not the dad, he was somewhere else waiting for me), all morphed into star-nosed moles. I woke up crying and I couldn't breathe. It felt so real. Now I have a stomachache—maybe I'm getting sick.

Yours truly,

THURSDAY, 8:00 A.M.

Kate,

I was hoping and praying I'd find your revise in my mailbox this morning.

I don't know what to say. I've already lied and told Oz the story was in—and it was great, and I'm on my period so stop bugging me every five minutes.

I know that's not your problem. That's mine. If I get fired, that's on me.

Just let me know? I feel like we've really gotten close these last few days, so just friend to friend, be straight with me. Also, just so you know, if you can't deliver as promised, we're going to be forced to swap in a photo spread of Woody Allen's greatest hits—you know, "Can we still love *Annie Hall*?"

(Btw there's a target between Mariel Hemingway's eyes. It's awful.)

Copyediting needs this by noon tomorrow. Drop-dead. Latest. Seriously. It's Friday, you know people are heading for the country. I'll stay as long as it takes—it's not like I'm dashing off to the Hamptons like everyone else—but I don't have a time machine.

I can't do this for you. I mean, if I need to I will—I mean, I can if you want. I can do it. I will write it if you want me to, but I don't think you want me to.

All I want is this: How old were you? Where were you? What time of day was it? What were you wearing? Skirt? Pants? Shorts? How dark was it? Was it before or after midnight? Were you wearing perfume? If so, what kind? When was the last time you'd showered? Could you smell yourself? Could anyone else smell you? Was he older than you or the same age? Was he handsome? Did you laugh at his jokes? Was there anything going through your mind? Were you happy for the attention? How did you react? When did you react? Did you react? If not, why not? What were you thinking? Could you think? When did everything change? If you saw yourself, was it like looking through the wrong end of a telescope? If you said anything, what did your voice sound like? Like a cartoon mouse? Is it possible that before you knew what was happening, it was nice? At first was it as unremarkable as bending a straw? Does your life break down into life before and after?

FRIDAY, 9:30 A.M.

We're almost there! Just one last thing—about the ending. We need some closure. Can you clarify, or simplify it?

You don't want the people you love, who love you, who are proud of you, to know you were raped, because they will believe it, and they will be heartbroken and they will be angry and full of guilt and helplessness, and they will want to do something, anything, their hands balled up in fists, but what? Hire a hitman? There's nothing they can do. They know it. And that will make them feel small and pathetic, and that pains you. You hate it. Their impotency embarrasses you. It will remind you of how small and pathetic and full of impotent rage you are. The fact that on top of all this, the people you love, who love you, who are proud of you, will also now feel awkward, possibly uncomfortable around you because you were raped when there's no reason for them to feel awkward or uncomfortable, after all, this was the whole point of keeping your mouth shut! It will be all the small things. Your mother, your sister, your friend will immediately change the channel when a man threatens a woman on TV, apologizing for not knowing it was coming, as though this were her fault. Your father, your brother, your friend, will hesitate before putting his hand on the small of your back to guide you across a slippery patch of ice, because he is afraid of startling you, of taking some liberty with your body—these men you love, reduced to their gender! This was the whole point of keeping your mouth shut! You didn't want the burden of their pity, or their guilt, or their sadness, or the burden of having to talk about it, you didn't want to wonder who among them wondered—full of shame but unable to help themselves, how much of this was your fault. You didn't want the responsibility of making everyone feel better about what happened to you. If you're not saying, "I'm fine," you are saying, "I'm sorry". You never envisioned this life for yourself. You don't know where you turned left instead of right, why it happened. All you know is that this is your story, and your story has a happy ending. This is a happy ending.

See what I mean, Kate?

The whole piece has been building to this moment! Come on! Just tell us the truth. Make us believe it.

ONE THOUSAND AND ONE NIGHTS

BY SAMANTHA HUNT

"I HATE RUNNING." MY OLDEST daughter might quit soccer.

I start to defend running, though running, to me, is always as in a dream, legs stuck in quicksand, lungs stiff with panic, the bad guy closing in. Why defend things I do not like? I tell my girl the truth. "I hate running, too."

*   *   *

When do the men come to you? They come to me at night. In the quiet, they find a way in, as if they'd been waiting in the foyer all day. Samantha will see you now. Which is to say, I let the men in, reckoning with the past. I don't sleep well and, through the long night, the men line up like planes for landing, a flight pattern of losers: the crotch-grabber on the night train; the frotteur on the Roman bus; the masturbator on the C local; the man in Grand Central; the man at the photo assistant interview; the guy in the Chevrolet; my older cousin's older boyfriend who slipped into my bed when I was fourteen; and the stranger jerking off beside me on a dark Santa Monica beach as I sang a slow, sad version of "Shattered," wearing my nutty song as a protective shroud of mental instability or at least a muffle to drown out the grunts and fleshy kneadings of him getting off on my fear.

When the men line up at night, I deal with the easy ones first, like a bureaucrat trying to clear my desk. The easy ones are the ones who got what they wanted. What did they want? That's harder to know. The rush of cruelty? The cold alarm of violence? Feeling like the big boss man? Ejaculation?

Control? Power? A rough grip on my soft parts? Proximity to gentleness, to a womb? Revenge? I don't know what the men wanted. But I'm quickly done with the ones who got what they were after. They are dismissed as sad sacks and losers. It's the ones whose attentions I escaped who present a stronger challenge in the night. These men remain an open file, a contract left unfulfilled. And that's how far I've normalized the abuse handed out by men.

A stranger in a green car pulled into my driveway. "Are you a good speller?" he asked.

"Yes." I was nine, playing in the yard.

"Can you spell *cat*?"

"C-A-T."

"Can you spell *pussy*?"

He wanted me to go somewhere with him. Where is that place he wanted to take me? Through the car window I saw what appeared to be a fake penis. I hadn't yet heard tales of erections. I thought, there is something really wrong with this guy's body. I ran.

Three Brits on holiday in Kinsale drank shots of Malibu, a coconut liquor named for a town that might be the opposite of Kinsale. They bought me a shot. One of them had canines like David Bowie's. They stood close. They touched me. I ran away that night, feeling victorious back at my hostel. Like a bank robber, I celebrated as if I had gotten away with a crime, only my crime was being a girl who wanted to be alone.

A man from Cork picked me up hitchhiking. I was dizzy with freedom, insistent on traveling the way I wanted. In his car danger was evident instantly. He looked as if he were actively trying in each moment to not cut me up and eat me. He licked his lips. I spoke about my parents and siblings. People love me. Please don't hurt me. I clutched a Swiss Army knife. Its blade was no longer than my index finger. I talked as to a wild animal, calming, humanizing. He stopped the car and I ran.

Does my escape from these men mean another woman had to take my place? A woman who couldn't run as fast as I could? I think about that often.

Because I ran, I'm left to write and rewrite versions of a narrative I did not begin. It's not even a story I like, yet I spend my nights imagining different possible endings. How I might have tripped, or slowed down, or decided to stay and enjoy the party a few moments too long.

Choose-Your-Own-Adventure, and by Adventure I suppose I mean assault. The Sultan and Scheherazade. I can't kill these men off because I don't know how their version of the story was intended to end.

My daughters are surrounded by good, calm, quiet, listening, kind men. The message has always been: Love all the people. But my oldest is eleven and soon I'll be remiss if I don't add an addendum about men. "Remember how I said love everyone? I didn't really mean *everyone*." I told her she could quit soccer if she wanted. Maybe that was a bad idea. But running was never a real solution.

On a freezing Vermont highway I had a flat tire. An older man in a pickup truck stopped. I asked him to drive to the next exit and call my boyfriend for help. He said no. He said he would drive *me* there. Please, I asked, just call him for me. No, he said, so I climbed into his cab, terrified. He spent the drive angry at me for not recognizing that he was a good guy, a kind father. I spent the drive wondering how I was supposed to know the difference. Was his goodness apparent in the style of his winter coat? The model of his car?

I was relieved. My daughter decided not to quit.

When the men come in the night, I'm going to ask them, How is it supposed to end?

The men will say, Wait a second. Who are you?

You know who I am.

I was drunk, they'll say.

You were but you're not now.

And they'll say, I don't know the ending.

I'll remind them how I, too, once didn't know the ending. How, because of them, I've now spent years of my life making up endings.

The men will say, I don't know what to say.

And I'll say, Yes. I know you don't. But I can wait. I've got all night.

CHANGING THE SUBJECT (DID IT EVER HAPPEN TO YOU?)

BY HONOR MOORE

I.

IT'S ALL TOO MUCH, she is saying, she has such misgivings, so many, you know, questions. This does not surprise me, as she is a contrarian.

But I am surprised at how quickly I begin to sweat, to feel woozy.

Well, I disagree. I mumbled this, looking across the table into my friend's implacable eyes.

You know, she says, all those men fired and no due process.

Has it ever happened to you? I ask her.

No, she says.

2.

It is 1969 and I am a graduate student. I am being escorted by the handsome department head into his office. He looks over his shoulder at the young men lounging in the anteroom: If we're not out in ten minutes, he says, bring the ice water. They all laugh.

3.

It happened to me four times, I say, expecting she will ask what it was that happened, but she just looks at me.

But you're all right, she says.

Not really, I answer. And change the subject.

4.

What would *all right* feel like if, when I was five, the male babysitter had not put his penis into my mouth? If when I was twenty-three and nude, the male student photographer had not also fucked me? If when I was twenty-four, the snow hadn't turned to blizzard, forcing an overnight stop when I gave a professor a ride to the city?

One room, he said, returning from the motel office.

Also *one bed*, all night me fighting him off in the sour dark.

Was it true there was only one room left?

5.

I was fourteen at the movies when anonymous fingers wormed into me, fedora and overcoat sliding away like a shadow.

My sister suspects her experiences were fewer because she is over six feet tall.

6.

What if the married man had not picked me up off the snow at an artists' colony and flirted with me?

If I had been *all right*, would I have fallen in love with him?

7.

Or did she say, You *turned out* all right?
   And which one of us changed the subject?

8.

As I begin to write, I become the subject.

9.

I wish I had kept count of the women killed, maimed,
raped, or abused since I began streaming video about
seven years ago.

10.

I thought that when I became sophisticated about sex,
I would learn how the ice water fit in.

11.

More like a comedy, 1969:

I was twenty-two, walking to my car across the summer theater parking lot, carrying at chest level a big office typewriter. I was wearing a mini-dress. What are you doing with that tonight? he asked. (I thought he meant the typewriter!)

He was staying in a hotel with other actors, and when we got to his room he took me to bed. There came a loud knock at the door and we disentangled. Another actor came in, sat down in a chair, and the two of them had a conversation as I lay there, silent.

When the actor left, we fucked for hours, said nothing. Decades later, he became an Oscar-winning movie star, and I ran into him somewhere.

It's been a long time, he said.

The typewriter, the silence, the sixties.

12.

Another of my sisters, not the tall one, thanked me once for recommending a very old chiropractor. Such a relief, she said; he doesn't ask me to take off my clothes.

13.

My father's mother told this story of her girlhood:

She was a bridesmaid, standing in a receiving line after a wedding. One of the groomsmen, instead of shaking her hand, embraced and kissed her. She hit him with her fist, knocking him to the floor.

The year was, say, 1906.

14.

I remember the beginning of Women's Liberation. I don't remember particular conversations, but I remember the confusion I would feel when a friend said she didn't need a women's movement.

Be careful how far you go with freedom, the old woman said; men can be violent. The year was 1971. The woman was the anthropologist Margaret Mead.

15.

A professor, when I was a year out of graduate school— this was before email, even answering machines, maybe 1969:

I dreamed you had become a very strong feminist and I would like to see you. I have called you many times and have not been able to reach you, so I am writing you a letter. I have read your poems and at least one of them is very good.

I remember talking to him at the table in my apartment, maybe about my poems. I did not move from the table until he left.

He is long dead, and I never saw him again.

Did he care one whit about my writing?

16.

I am wearing a pink cotton Marimekko dress, short and sleeveless. It is spring and I am twenty-three, and my lover is eighteen years older. I had pursued him. I believed he was a genius. He wore Italian cashmere turtlenecks.

I don't know about those black underpants, Pussy, he said. Better pull the skirt down. Pretty dark up there.

17.

In the dark of memory, I turn toward the future.

A million pink pussycat hats in the snow.

APOLOGIA

BY DONIKA KELLY

I.

IT BEGINS AS NO apologia does: with an apology \\ a desire to
offer something in return \\ for what was taken \\ under
the black walnut tree \\ over the maggot fruit \\ or in the peach
room \\ the door with no knob \\ the door, unpainted \\ or in
the kitchen \\ the linoleum worn and gold \\ or in my parents'
bedroom \\ or in the den \\ or in the dining room \\ or in the
living room \\ or anywhere \\ we've been alone \\ *is his hat* \\ *in
his hand* \\ he doesn't wear a hat \\ *I meant it metaphorically* \\
still he apologized \\ still he said he was sorry \\ still he offered
me anything I wanted \\ he asked what I wanted \\ but what had
he taken \\ what \\ what \\ what could he give me in return?

II.

Even the second act begins
with an apology. He sits
in the passenger seat
of my 1985 Honda Prelude.
I am looking forward,
toward the shed of the house
I used to live in, a house
over two thousand miles away
from where he [   ] me.

Inside, my mama is spinning,
a tornado smashing
her children into refuse.
Who remembers
when last she was sober?
Who remembers?

Outside, in my car, the one headlight
pulled up with bungee cord and hook,
I ask my dad, I say
[

                              ]?

He looks forward.
He is too big for the car.
His hands are scarred and calloused.
They haven't been clean
for longer than I remember.

I remember how high
he would throw the ball.

I remember him picking me up
when I was asleep,

how safe and then unsafe I felt.
All the ways he carried me away.

He is sorry for [   ] me,
though he will not admit
to [   ] me to anyone
outside this car. Not my aunts
and great-aunts. Not my grandfather.
Not my mama. Although all of them know
what he has done. Although each believes
every man capable of such a thing.

Still, this is how he convinces me,
for the second time:
this is no apologia but an apology.

No argument in defense
of [   ] me. I take
what little he gives because I believe
the lowered head, the strained voice,
his hands so dirty in his own lap.

III.

The small shames \\ are the hardest to say \\ we went to the toy store \\ I picked out a small model plane \\ the rubber cement \\ I remember the paints were too expensive \\ so \\ no paint \\ *what did my brother and sister get \\ no way I got a toy \\ and them, nothing* \\ Paperboy on the radio \\ Too $hort \\ the sun shining on our way to the mall \\ on the way back \\ fucking California sun \\ the plane the only thing I could think to say \\ I had wanted it \\ or something like it \\ for so long \\ so frivolous \\ the plane \\ with no paint \\ that I put together the rest of the afternoon \\ what he gave me in return

IV.

Now the apologia, poorly argued:
a statement he would never say to me

because we have not spoken to each other
in over five years, and we have not spoken

not because he [   ] me,
but because, when my mama died

and the doctors brought her back,
after he cried and cried and cried

for what was lost and the long arduous
road ahead, he brought my mama

a twelve-pack of beer and left for the night,
and the night after and many more besides.

Which means he did not walk into my bedroom
unbidden, did not stand just inside

the open door, a body full of sway and swagger,
the beer ruining his breath, he did not set

his wheeling gaze in my direction to tell me:

> *I am not || sorry || I liked it || I would || do*
> *it again || if I had the chance || again || if I*
> *had the chance || again || I am not sorry || I*
> *am not sorry || not || sorry || not sorry.*

But I'll ask:
What kind of argument is this?
What warranting?
What evidence?
What pathos what logos what ethos?

What else but a drunken slurring
of a god-turned-man in some flickering light.

And besides, who asked what he wanted?

A GOOD MAN IS HARD TO FIND

BY HAFIZAH GETER

I'VE BEEN ROOFIED. I'VE been prevented from leaving a dorm room late at night until I gave in to oral sex—though I was assured afterwards that the whole thing was in good fun. A friend who I swore to God was safe stuck his hands down my pants, repeatedly, in a bar full of people, in spite of all the times I said *stop*—*no*. We never spoke of it, but what else was I supposed to do but hug him back when he said 'It's so good to see you' a year later at the Charlotte airport? I've feigned deafness when white men in bars leaned in to ask me for *a little strange*, their tongues wetting each word, each lip, the tips of their fingers. I've played along in the dark when things got weird, hard to predict, deciding the safest bet was to go with the devil I knew.

I've overheard good men ask *How much did she drink?* and *What was she wearing*? I have watched Men Who Would Never say nothing to the Men Who Did. I've tried to be patient with good men who are utterly shocked that so many women have been abused in so many ways by so many men. A fact so obvious I wonder what it must feel like to wear that much privilege.

Increasingly, I find myself sitting across from good men who, while they are concerned about the safety of women and the predation of men, are equally, if not more, mortally afraid for themselves. It seems even the good men can feel the invisible throne of patriarchy slipping, can sense that when it goes it will take something even from them, despite their goodness.

Because of the size and unstoppable growth of the internet, people of color, women, and others long marginalized are finding platforms to amplify their voices and their stories. Stories that matter. Stories so damning in their truth that simply uttering them destabilizes institutions of oppression and power. The sheer amount of muscle true stories can hold is why we ban books.

Surveying the women around me, I've found there isn't a single one among us who hasn't said *yes* just because we've been unsure of what might happen if we said *no*. That we all share this is a fact that surprises none of us. Though many of us are women with master's degrees, doctorates, MFAs, we are also women who cover the broad spectrum of class and race. We are women of institutions, a fact that affords us certain privileges. But no amount of privilege can spare a woman from the bruises of patriarchy.

From Harvey Weinstein to Matt Lauer, from Louis C.K. to Al Franken to Charlie Rose, I hear so many good men asking questions thinly veiled by rhetoric: *But surely you're worried about this social media justice? When does the punishment outgrow the crime?* Now that powerful men are increasingly being held accountable for their abuses, more men than ever are engaging with the issue of sexual assault. It's not a coincidence. I'm weary from hearing so many good men say more about their concerns around abusive men being outed on social media than I've ever heard them say about the lack of laws to protect women. I've never heard the good men in my life ask how all the women with untested rape kits are faring, or whether all the women who have had to foot the bill to get their rape kits tested could afford the price.

When the good men around me voice their concerns about the problem of "Twitter justice," they seem genuinely surprised when I ask them to imagine planting a lie ten, fifteen, twenty years in advance. To imagine strategically scattering that lie among people around you so that in ten, fifteen, twenty years you have outcry witnesses. I ask them if their past is credible enough to have a journalist tear through it looking for holes. As a black woman, I know this line of questioning, this jive, very well. I know how when the marginalized find too much stage the pitch of our voice is accused of being threatening. How when we march peacefully we are written off as rioters. How we kneel and suddenly it's demanded that we stand.

For hundreds of years women have been relying on our whisper networks to warn us of dangerous men. The best we can do is hope our network warns us in time. But when you're pinned under someone else's power, warnings often come too late.

Sometimes, I want to ask the good men in my life to imagine walking outside and having their every day begin with a threat from the kind of man who wants you to know he knows where you live. To go to work and receive creepy advances on top of being allowed to take home only seventy-nine cents of your dollar if you're white, sixty-three if you're black. To imagine trying to keep track of—to anticipate—all of the consequences of the word *no*.

No woman wants Twitter justice more than she wants to see her abuser held accountable. I want to remind good men who are suddenly scared of swarms of false accusations that educating, managing, leading, legislating, enforcing, and prosecuting as though we believe in a woman's bodily sovereignty has always been the solution.

The thing about oppression—sexual, racial, or otherwise—is that it convinces you that the polite thing, the safe thing, is to keep its secrets. The thing about patriarchy is that it convinces you that even a bad man is a good man, and that a good man is hard to find. From movies to politics to music, culture *trains* women in the scarcity of good men, so we accept the idea of "good" in all its misshapen forms. This is how patriarchy convinces women to stay—to take the abuse, the neglect, the punch.

Mornings before work, my girlfriend scoops coffee into our percolator and puts WNYC on our Bluetooth. One day she says, *Ugh, so much rape.* For too long, our mornings have been filled with sexual assault, with women's uphill battle against a cultural and political disregard for us. There has been "grab 'em by the pussy," debates on how long is fair for an eighty-one-year-old Bill Cosby to serve in prison for decades of drugging women. There has been Sherman Alexie, Junot Diaz, Brett Kavanagh—supposedly good men from all walks of life, dethroned. The bar for male morality seems so low, the one for women unattainably high. As a queer black woman I live in a state of heightened perception. I live at the intersection of a crash. And at night I pray not to God, but to women. I hear the rumble, the din slowly turning itself up. Our stories are rising. Like any marginalized group attempting to break its chains, it is our stories that make us so utterly dangerous to white patriarchal institutions. Our safety is a fiction. The danger we live in, the secret we will no longer keep.

BUT WE WILL WIN

BY SHELLY ORIA

THE FIRST MAN I KILLED was probably a sweetheart. He didn't say anything dirty or try to start a fight, like some of the others. He just asked if I knew her, the woman in the picture. But I'm getting ahead of myself. Roxie used to tell me: you talk like whoever's listening already knows what you're about to say. I always wanted to ask: why shouldn't I? Now it's too late.

From what I understand, Roxie's father named her Roxie—just Roxie, not short for anything—because he was Greek and in his language the name means star, or something close to star. He was a poet, possibly a bad one. On the day she was born he glared at her for hours through the viewing room glass, a baby among babies, and wrote a poem about the newborn who shone like a star in his sky. Later, his wife read the poem, and perhaps because she had nothing else to say, she offered they name the child after the title.

When Roxie told me this story—the red of her hair a dark brown that day, a color-trick it played when cut short, and her eyes made softer somehow by the new edges—I asked whether her father wrote the poem in Greek or in English. We were sharing ice cream that was supposedly made of lemonade, a hip new import from Switzerland or maybe Sweden. On the bench outside the fake ice cream parlor, Roxie gave me a look that suggested my question was dumb. She did that sometimes: at random moments all kinds of feelings from the previous week or month— perhaps feelings that had gone unexpressed because Roxie always worked hard to stay sweet—suddenly found their way to her eyebrows, her lips, the creases of her forehead.

She seemed unaware of her face whenever it responded before she did, so I learned early on to smile and wait. When her words caught up, they often changed the subject. *There's no way this is actually lemonade, right?* Roxie said that day. *It's the best thing I've ever put in my mouth.*

I made a pamphlet after Roxie died. The front features a picture of her and the two dates bookending her life. It says, *This woman died of sexual harassment.* The back cites statistics: *Tens of thousands of women die of sexual harassment in this country every day*, that sort of thing. Of course the number refers to deaths small and big, quiet and loud, personal and public, but the brochure doesn't go into that sort of detail.

My point was to bring attention to the larger issue. Roxie would have been disappointed in anything less. *The story of a woman is the story of a nation,* she'd have said. *When we keep our stories so small that people can't see the world through them, we fail.* Or perhaps she wouldn't have said that at all, perhaps that's just me assuming again that my listener knows what I'm about to say. But if I commemorated the life of one fatality without lamenting the larger war, who would I even be?

I still use my pamphlet sometimes: situate myself on a street corner not unlike the one in my old town where Roxie was killed, shout out some truths, distribute that carefully crafted piece of glossy paper to passersby. But not often. It causes friction with my new girlfriend, who believes it's unsafe. *There are men out there just waiting for an excuse to rape*, she says.

She's right, of course. We have seen our world turn against us. We have seen women's bodies violated, then jailed for the crimes they suffered. We have seen laws modified to protect the strong. But what my girlfriend really means is, *And then you'll off somebody again and then we'll have to move again.* She'll never say it, because she doesn't want to appear jealous of a dead girl. Instead, she hides my weapons when she thinks I'm rageful. The good knife behind the meat in the freezer, the gun in the laundry basket. *Silly girl,* I say and pull her close. *You think I need anything more than these?* I show her my hands.

Roxie and I never even officially dated, but I would have thrown myself in front of that truck if it meant saving her life. And one night I was dumb enough or drunk enough to admit that truth to my girlfriend. *Why?* she asked, assuming the casual tone of a woman not threatened in the least by her lover's willingness to die for another lover. I said I didn't know why, not to avoid an answer— though it did hit me, right as I confessed, that this was one honesty I would live to regret—but because I truly had no idea. I didn't mention that I knew it right away, too: that my willingness to die for Roxie wasn't something that developed over time, but something I felt the first day we met. That day, at the park where I used to play with my dog, I watched her with the two kids I later learned she nannied—twins, a boy and a girl, who kept shouting words they should not have been shouting, *shit shit sex butt*, Roxie's gentle face looking at once appalled and amused— and thought: *I would die to save this woman's life.* A foreshadow? A warning from my unconscious mind of what lay ahead? I doubt it. I think we all have people like that, walking the great earth, and if we're lucky we meet one of them and we immediately know; it's as simple as a pair of pants in need of laundry: *I would give my life for yours.*

*　　*　　*

Designing my pamphlet was an elaborate process. The font choice alone took months. I kept staring at different letter shapes, tracing their movement on the page with my finger. *Is this one Roxie?* I would ask. *Is that one? Or that one? Or that one?* Sometimes I'd hear her pick a font, then laugh. *Just kidding!* She was taunting me because she didn't believe my activism mattered. *It's over*, she'd say in my head, meaning maybe her life, or maybe the whole world.

The street where it happened isn't a busy one. I've always wondered what role the quiet played in Roxie's death. Because, well, imagine this: the same Roxie, the same man, the same *Come over here, baby*, the same *look at that ass move*, the same guttural sound of a hungry animal. But one difference: cars roaring. Would Roxie still run away from him and into traffic? I try not to think about it.

Another thing I try not to think about is Roxie in the hospital. She was out of the ICU and seemed okay—bruised and shaken up, but not dying. Reality is a tricky force; its credibility allows it to get away with all kinds of deception. I was in the cafeteria getting a chai latte when she collapsed. A nurse came to get me. I don't remember what this nurse said, but I remember she called Roxie "Rosie." I remember the room looking pale, all the color sucked out. *Are you okay?* the nurse asked. She grabbed my arm, a tight grip that said only an asshole would let herself faint in this moment. I remember wanting to punch this nurse. I remember knowing she was the last woman I would ever look at without wondering if her body, like Roxie's, might be hiding its quiet bleeding from me. This was how I learned: we are always dying.

My girlfriend pointed out that designing the brochure may not be the real challenge, that I may not be ready to take my story to the streets just yet. To prove her wrong, I blindfolded myself one day and chose a font. But on my first day out there I realized my girlfriend had been right. Anger is a tricky force, too; when coerced into disguise, it grows stronger.

Most people who approached me while I was distributing pamphlets—right from the start, before I ever killed anyone—tried to figure out what my deal was: why I was standing on a corner with a stack of brochures. Was I some kind of crazy woman? I developed strategies to redirect their thinking, to get them to focus on the issue, but I usually failed.

What happened on the day of my first kill was that I let my failure get to my head. In other words, I acted like a man. The man in front of me—skin the color of marshmallow, bones long and skinny—wore a suit but carried a gym bag, which I found strange. *So was she your friend... or, like, how'd you know her?* he asked me. I asked him what difference it made. I asked him what it meant, in his mind, to "know" somebody. It's just a dumb thing people say, isn't it, as hollow as anything made of language. Knowing another human being is impossible.

He considered this for a moment; as I said, he was probably a sweetheart. But I was already too worked up. I pushed him—not even hard at first, just hard enough. He folded, lost his balance. You see, the first move is special: what rises to meet you is never real muscle, only a man's instinct.

Learning that for the first time made me smile.

The next moment is quite different—the shock on their face, the shame of being hit by a girl. He was on the ground now. If you're skilled, you can use that shock, those milliseconds of inaction. I wasn't skilled yet, but I'd seen some moves. I kicked his head hard. After that it's pure intuition: you let your body lead you. My body led me to use the man's tie.

Afterwards, I hovered over his body as it fluttered between worlds. *It's a war now*, I whispered, *and wars kill many innocents.* I looked at him to be sure. He was gone. I closed one of his eyelids, left the other one open. *We didn't start the war,* I told the winking lifeless man, *but we will win.*

When I come home bloodied, my girlfriend washes me up. She burns my clothes. Then she reaches for me, puts my fingers deep inside her and starts to move. Sometimes we're upright when she does this, not even in bed yet, as if her body can't bear the wait. I know she'll cry when she comes. In the dark she'll ask me to choose life, choose hope. What she means by life and hope is that she's sick of hiding from uniformed men. She means that if I keep going, one day I'll get caught. And then what, she asks me. *Then what?* When she asks me this, I take her words and turn them around like a mirror. *Then what?* I ask her.

My girlfriend knows what I'm really asking. I ask her this question every day. I ask myself. I ask the earth, the air, the nothing and everything in which we all swim. I'm asking you. What would it take for you to join me?

CONTRIBUTORS

SHELLY ORIA is the author of *New York 1, Tel Aviv 0* (Farrar, Straus and Giroux, 2014), which earned nominations for a Lambda Literary Award and the Edmund White Award for Debut Fiction, among other honors. Recently she coauthored a digital novella, *CLEAN,* commissioned by WeTransfer and *McSweeney's*, which received two Lovie Awards from the International Academy of Digital Arts and Sciences. Oria's fiction has appeared in the *Paris Review* and elsewhere; has been translated to other languages; and has won a number of awards. Oria lives in Brooklyn, New York, where she has a private practice as a life and creativity coach. Her website is www.shellyoria.com

KAITLYN GREENIDGE's debut novel is *We Love You, Charlie Freeman* (Algonquin Books), one of the *New York Times* Critics' Top 10 Books of 2016. She is currently a contributing writer for the *New York Times*. She lives in Brooklyn, NY.

MELISSA FEBOS is the author of the memoir, *Whip Smart*, and the essay collection, *Abandon Me*. Her work has recently appeared in *Tin House, Granta, Sewanee Review*, the *Believer,* and the *New York Times*.

SYREETA MCFADDEN is a writer and professor of English at the Borough of Manhattan Community College, City University of New York. Her work has appeared in the poetry anthology, *Break Beat Poets 2: Black Girl Magic*, the *Atlantic, New York Times Magazine, Elle*, the *Guardian*, and *BuzzFeed News*. She is currently writing a book-length collection of essays about African Americans in the Middle West.

REBECCA SCHIFF's collection *The Bed Moved* came out from Knopf in 2016 and was a finalist for an *LA Times* Book Prize for First Fiction. Her stories have appeared in *Electric Literature, n+1*, the *Guardian, Washington Square*, and *BuzzFeed*. She lives in Eugene, Oregon.

DIANA SPECHLER is the author of the novels *Who by Fire* and *Skinny*, of the *New York Times* column *Going Off*, and of a forthcoming memoir. Her work has appeared in *GQ,*

Esquire, BBC Travel, the *Wall Street Journal, Harper's, Glimmer Train Stories, Harper's Bazaar*, and many other publications.

HOSSANNAH ASUNCION is the author of *Object Permanence* and has received fellowships from Kundiman, The Poetry Society of America, and The Laundromat Project. She loves her writing composition students at the Borough of Manhattan Community College. She lives in Bed-Stuy, Brooklyn with her wife, daughter, and cat.

NELLY REIFLER is the author of *See Through* and *Elect H. Mouse State Judge*. Her work has been published in *McSweeney's, Lucky Peach, jubilat*, and *Story*, among others, and read aloud on Selected Shorts and at Audible. She lives in New York City and teaches at Sarah Lawrence College.

COURTNEY ZOFFNESS won the Sunday Times EFG Short Story Award, the Arts & Letters Creative Nonfiction Prize, an Emerging Writers Fellowship from The Center for Fiction, and two MacDowell Colony fellowships. She's published work in several journals and anthologies, and was a notable essayist in *Best American Essays 2018*.

QUITO ZIEGLER is a cultural producer with several film projects in the works, including an all-ages TV show about the future, when society has transformed and the world is a better place. They are a founding member of the WRRQ Collective, an intergenerational community of queer/trans artists and activists who make art and food together for visual resistance and collective healing.

MECCA JAMILAH SULLIVAN, Ph.D. is author of *Blue Talk and Love (stories)*, and winner of the Judith Markowitz Award for LGBTQ Writers, the Charles Johnson Fiction Award, and honors from Bread Loaf, the NEA, and others. She is Assistant Professor of English at Bryn Mawr College. Her fiction and scholarship have been published widely.

JOLIE HOLLAND is an American songwriter, bandleader, multi-instrumentalist, singer, producer, and author. Her albums include *The Living and the Dead*, *Pint of Blood*, and *Wine Dark Sea*. In a review on National Public Radio, critic Stephen Thompson lauded her music for combining blues, rock, jazz, and soul into "a sound that lands halfway between dusty rural Americana and grimy New

York art-rock." Holland's essays have been published by University of Chicago Press and by Talk House. Her lyrics were used as the epigraph in Kerouac's first novel *The Haunted Life*.

LYNN MELNICK is the author of the poetry collections *Landscape with Sex and Violence* and *If I Should Say I Have Hope*.

CAITLIN DELOHERY is a writer and editor from Portland, Oregon. She is a MacDowell Colony fellow (2009, 2019), and she's currently at work on a memoir about murder, sexual assault, and silence.

PAISLEY REKDAL is the author of eight books, most recently, *Nightingale* (Copper Canyon Press), which re-writes many of the myths in Ovid's *The Metamorphoses*. *Appropriate: A Provocation*, a book-length essay examining cultural appropriation, is forthcoming from W.W. Norton. Her work has received a Guggenheim Fellowship, the Amy Lowell Poetry Traveling Fellowship, a Fulbright Fellowship, and other honors.

CAITLIN DONOHUE is a freelance writer living in Mexico City. She writes about reggaeton for *Remezcla* and *FACT* magazine and on cannabis for *High Times*, in addition to other publications. Read her work and follow her on Twitter.

GABRIELLE BELLOT is a staff writer for Literary Hub. Her work has appeared in the *New Yorker*, the *New York Times*, the *Atlantic*, the *Cut*, *Guernica*, *Tin House*, *Electric Literature*, the *New York Review of Books*, the *Paris Review Daily*, and many other places. She holds both an MFA and PhD in Fiction from Florida State University. She lives in Brooklyn.

KARISSA CHEN has essays and fiction in *Catapult, Longreads, PEN America, Gulf Coast* and *Guernica*, among others. A Fulbright Fellow and NJ Council on the Arts grants recipient, she is also the editor-in-chief at *Hyphen* and Fiction Editor at *The Rumpus*. She is currently working on a novel.

ELISSA SCHAPPELL is the author of two books of fiction, *Blueprints for Building Better Girls*, and *Use Me*, a runner-up for the PEN Hemingway Award. She is also a journalist, essayist, and book reviewer, as well as a Contributing Editor at *Vanity Fair*, and a Founding-editor of *Tin House*.

SAMANTHA HUNT is the author of *The Dark Dark: Stories, and three novels. Mr. Splitfoot* is a ghost story. *The Invention of Everything Else* is about the life of inventor Nikola Tesla. *The Seas*, Hunt's first novel, was republished by Tin House Books in 2018. Hunt is the recipient of a 2017 Guggenheim Fellowship and the Bard Fiction Prize.

HONOR MOORE's new memoir *Our Revolution: A Mother and Daughter at Midcentury* will be published on what would have been her mother's 97th birthday, March 12, 2020. Her first collection of poems *MEMOIR* (1988) will be reissued as a classic collection by Carnegie Mellon in October, 2019.

DONIKA KELLY is the author of *Bestiary* (Graywolf 2016) and the chapbook *Aviarium* (500 Places 2017). She is a Cave Canem Graduate Fellow, and winner the 2018 Kate Tufts Discovery Prize. She is an Assistant Professor teaching creative writing at Baruch College.

Born in Zaria, Nigeria, HAFIZAH GETER's poetry and prose have appeared in the *New Yorker*, *Tin House*, *Narrative* magazine, *Gulf Coast*, *Boston Review*, *Los Angeles Review of Books*, *McSweeney's*, and *Longreads*, among others. She is an editor for Little A from Amazon Publishing and serves on the poetry committee for the Brooklyn Book Festival.

ACKNOWLEDGMENTS

To the women who came forward in October 2017, to the countless women who've come forward before and since, to every person who's ever said #MeToo on social media, to every person who shared their story with even one friend: thank you. This book is for you.

Dr. Christine Blasey Ford: never in my life have I felt such deep gratitude to a woman I've never met.

Tarana Burke, thank you for doing the hard work before anyone else did.

To the fierce writers and artists whose work is featured in these pages: thank you for your brilliance, and thank you for your courage. Thank you, too, for your patience with me along the way.

Kristina Kearns: thank you for your vision and for trusting me with it. Your skill and spirit live in every word of this book.

It's common knowledge that anyone with a @mcsweeneys.net email also possesses ungodly levels of skill and talent; I've never figured out if the prowess came with the address or the other way around.

Amanda Uhle, a wonderwoman in every sense: thank you for all your superpowers. I'm not prone to hyperbole, so this is meant as a dry and factual statement: I've never enjoyed working with anyone as much as I've enjoyed working with you.

Sunra Thompson: your artistry never ceases to amaze me. Dan Weiss: thank you for always saying yes. Daniel Levin Becker, language conductor: thank you for the music. Rita Bullwinkel, your generosity and support in the early days of this project meant more than you know.

Jon Maunder, thank you for believing in this book and chasing all the magic on its behalf.

Making an anthology is a unique kind of collaboration work, a multi-legged creature trying to learn how to dance. Thank you to all my collaborators, past and present, who've trained me in the art of creative space-sharing: Alice Sola Kim, Hannah Assadi, Alexander Borinsky, Tanya Gill, Alon Pdut, Michael Mayer, Robert Lopez, Matthew Baker, and the one-and-only Nelly Reifler.

PJ Mark, I'm always and forever indebted to you.

Emily Bell, I can't imagine my writing life—or my life life for that matter—without your ever-present support and your faith in me.

Elizabeth Reichert, if I'm even half the writing wife to you that you are to me, I'm doing a stellar job.

So many good souls have already supported this book and helped spread the word of its impending birth. Thank you: Ashley Judd, Tabitha St. Bernard-Jacobs, Jami Attenberg, Joanna Klink, Julie Stevenson, Caroline Keys, Deb Olin Unferth, Rachel Heng, Kristen Millares Young, Sally Franson, Sharma Shields, Julie Buntin, Kelly Luce, Lydia Kiesling, Alexander Chee, Victor LaValle, Laura van den Berg.

The only time in the past two years when I was able to keep up with this book and experience continuous commitment to another project was the spring I spent in the woods of New Hampshire. The MacDowell Colony remains my favorite place on this Earth.

To my hearts Diana Spechler, Galit Lotan, Courtney Zoffness, Kerry Carnahan, Georgia Wall, Tali Herskowitz, Maya Michaeli, and Gretchen Jones: thank you for holding me extra tight this past year.

And finally, to my parents, Eliya and Avi Oria, and my sister, Dana Oria: that the three of you are my family is by far my biggest windfall in this life.